THE COMPLEAT CRICKETER

THE COMPLEAT CRICKETER

Jonathan Rice

ILLUSTRATED BY
WILLIAM RUSHTON

JAVELIN BOOKS
POOLE · NEW YORK · SYDNEY

First published in the UK 1985 by Blandford Press,
Link House, West Street, Poole, Dorset, BH15 1LL
This edition published in Javelin Books May 1986

FOR

JAN,

WITHOUT WHOM
I WOULDN'T NEED
THE MONEY.

Distributed in the United States by
Sterling Publishing Co., Inc.,
2 Park Avenue, New York, NY 10016

Distributed in Australia by
Capricorn Link (Australia) Pty Ltd.
PO Box 665, Lane Cove, NSW 2066

British Library Cataloguing in Publication Data

Rice, Jonathan
  The compleat cricketer.—2nd ed.
  1. Cricket—Anecdotes, facetiae, satire, etc.
  I. Title
  796.35'8'0207   GV919

ISBN 0 7137 1862 5

Typeset by Graphicraft Typesetters Limited, Hong Kong

Printed in Great Britain by
Cox and Wyman Ltd, Reading, Berks.

CONTENTS

FOREWORD BY DAVID GOWER

Some time in the middle of the summer of 1984, after close of play one day during the Sri Lanka Test Match — which, contrary to universal hopes and expectations, was not progressing any more in England's favour than had the previous five against the West Indies — I took the obvious course as Captain of this beleaguered side: I headed for one of those very convenient hospitality boxes in the Tavern Stand, confident at least that the host, one T.M.B. Rice, would be pleased to see me and, with his usual band of resident experts, would be able to offer solace certainly and, most importantly, refreshment. I knew he would restore my sense of priorities by bringing me up to date with the latest successes and failures of his own Heartaches C.C. All of this happened, of course: a fresh bottle of dry white was opened, Tony Lewis did the sympathy bit, and Jo Rice decided the time was right to take advantage and enquire if I would pen the foreword to this epic volume.

It is only when you sit down to try and start a foreword that you begin to wonder where or how you start it. Having achieved that, I can how go on to reveal that here we have a book aimed at the true fanatic of whatever standard, who will at last discover the innermost secrets of this game as described by Jo Rice and as illustrated by Willie Rushton. It probably says all that on the cover anyway, and I just hope that the true fanatic finds the book and buys it! Both Jo and Willie are of that same ilk, and I have had the privilege to play alongside Mr Rushton, in Berlin of all places, where one of his more telling contributions was to suggest no-balling ventriloquist Ken Wood for throwing his voice.

Between them they have a great love and fascination for cricket and have accordingly produced a cracking book to amuse us all.

Most aspects of the game are covered (except how to write forewords for cricket books) and it is left to you to decide whether or not to follow the advice herein. All I will reveal as the professional here is that the principles for selection on the England winter tour appear to be rather different from the guidelines set down for the High Dudgeon C.C. Annual Grand Tour.

The Compleat Cricketer is to be greatly enjoyed — please do!

ACKNOWLEDGEMENTS

A large number of people share the responsibility for getting this book out of my head and on to the bookshelves, and they need not imagine they will get away with anonymity. I name the guilty men.

Willie Rushton has cartooned superbly, and now is the only man in history to have combined with both my brother and me on separate cricket books. His career can only go upwards from here. David Gower, captain of Leicestershire and England, has written a foreword as elegant as his batting. I only hope he has not taken the advice within these covers too much to heart. John Newth has edited my efforts with the patience one has come to expect from a Gloucestershire supporter, and my wife Jan has typed most of it, interpreting my spidery longhand with consistent accuracy.

Finally, I want to acknowledge the efforts of all the club and village cricketers I have played with and against, who have unwittingly made contributions to this book. In 1973 my brother Tim founded Heartaches C.C., upon whose misadventures some passages are unashamedly based. Saltwood C.C. is a Kent village side of far greater vintage, but their ability to break deck chairs, eat three teas and maintain one of the loveliest grounds I have played on shows the very spirited enjoyment of the game that continues there and amongst all our opponents in South and East Kent.

1
TAKE GUARD

Once upon a time sports were what schoolchildren, both small and overgrown, got up to, and most of us were able to abandon all pretence of physical activity as soon as we left that stage behind us and went out into the cruel world to earn our keep. Now it has all changed. (Let us leave on one side the politically controversial opinion that many school-leavers are no longer presented with opportunities to earn their keep, as this slim volume is not intended as a manifesto for would-be Prime Ministers. Any overthrows referred to from now on will be of the cricketing rather than the governmental variety.) What has changed, as far as you and I of the mature proletariat are concerned, is that no longer can we state, hand on heart, that we gave up sports when we gave up school. We gave up exams, we gave up school dinners and we gave up smoking behind the bike sheds, but try as we might public opinion will not let us give up being sporty. Sports are to the 1980s what incense and flowers were to the 1960s — the image and essence of youth and fashion. So now that even the most diehard of the sixties' flower children has thrown out his bell bottom trousers and his beads, a nation of ageing hippies has turned to sport for its physical and spiritual salvation.

The sport that is one of the most turned to, the Maharishi of Sports, is Cricket. It combines all the virtues that the reluctant athlete requires, and it embraces the sporting duffer as easily and completely as the super-hero. Cricket can be gentle or violently physical, it can be long-lasting or over in an hour or so, but if you go about it the right way, it will never be unprofitable or dull. It is also almost entirely unavoidable, so, unless you wish your life to be one long catalogue of failure and social ostracism, you need to know how to succeed at cricket. You need to have cricket unzipped so that you can read its entrails and win.

I would not like it to be thought that I am exaggerating in pointing out that cricket is unavoidable, because it is. Many a foolhardy man (and woman) has gone through adult life believing that cricket is there to be sidestepped, but as time goes by the old footwork tends to get a bit less dazzling and cricket gets you in the end.

Consider the fate of one Ricardo Romero, who was not even English and therefore could have been excused for believing that cricket, of which he had never heard, would not form part of the colourful tapestry of his life. How foolhardy can one be? Ricardo's first major mistake was meeting an English girl in Benidorm and subsequently marrying her. He compounded this first error by coming to live in England, and taking a job teaching Spanish at a language school on the South Coast. Over the years, Ricardo's wife presented him with three children and the school became noted for the standard of its Spanish teaching, thanks almost entirely to Ricardo's efforts. He was a happy, successful family man with a bright future ahead of him. Then one summer the school employed a young Englishman to teach English Culture to the European students who swarmed across the Channel for a summer of learning and liberation, and Señor Romero's world started to fall apart. The young Englishman, whom we shall call Paul Chester to protect the innocent, enjoyed his cricket, and as part of his course of English Culture for the pretty French, German and Swedish ladies under his tutorial guidance, he decided to organise a cricket match. This, he felt, would give the students a chance to savour something peculiarly English in our culture, and would also give his biceps and all-round athleticism a fine opportunity for exhibition to an admiring audience. Once the decision was taken, poor Ricardo's whole existence was put at risk. The match that was organised was six-a-side (it was not a very big school) between the Teachers and the Administrative Staff. The rules were simple. Ten overs a side, each player except the wicket-keeper to bowl two overs.

To give him his due, Ricardo tried to escape, but he had

reckoned without the inevitability of cricket at some stage in every English resident's life. The unfeeling Paul Chester selected Ricardo for his team. This was not altogether surprising as there were only seven teachers at the school of whom one was sporting a broken leg from a cricketing accident earlier in the season, when he had tripped on a doughnut as he came down the pavilion steps after tea. The fact that Ricardo had been brought up on pelota and bull-fighting was seen as only a minor inconvenience. Because he clearly did not know too much about bowling, he was selected as wicket-keeper and the match began. The students crowded round the boundary as the perfectly-formed, bronzed figure of Paul Chester ran in to bowl the first ball of the match.

It was a good length ball, pitching just outside the off stump and moving away from the batsman, Doug Lee the accountant. He played half forward and the snick was heard all round the ground. All eyes turned to the wicket-keeper, poised for the catch. Unfortunately, the wicket-keeper had not himself attended the course on English Culture and did not understand that we take our cricket seriously. With a flourish, Ricardo pulled his bright red gloves away from the ball at the last second and shouted 'Olé' as the ball sped to the boundary for four. He smiled broadly and waved a red handkerchief at the bowler, who ran towards him as furiously as any charging bull ever aimed at El Cordobes.

'Don't worry, Paul,' said Ricardo. 'Next time I cut off the batter's ears and present them to the crowd.'

'Batsman, not batter', was the only reply.

The rest of the match failed to add much to the general level of European understanding of our culture, but for the Teachers' wicket-keeper it was the turning point in his life. In the Common Room where once he had been a friend and respected colleague, he was now just another foreigner. Furthermore his students realised that what had occurred on the cricket pitch had in some inscrutable British way been the wrong thing to do, and they treated their Spanish professor with less deference than hitherto. Spurned by his colleagues and laughed at by his students, Señor Romero began the long slide into anonymity. When last heard of,

OLE!

'... the wicket-keeper had not attended the course on English Culture...'

he was a deck-chair attendant in Marbella, swigging Cyprus sherry behind the rubble of half-built hotels and cursing the day that leather first met willow. The moral of this little story is that a man ignores cricket at his peril. Like telephone answering machines and Pay As You Enter buses, cricket will one day, if only for a brief period, assume a central position in your life, and you had best understand how it works.

There have been other people in this life who have assumed that, in confronting cricket, attack is the best form of defence. Unfortunately, as many an aggressive batsman has discovered over the years, this policy does not usually work for long. At some stage circumstances will conspire against you and you will be found wanting. It is no good merely being able to talk about cricket, to write about it or to be involved in an administrative capacity with the game. At some stage, somebody will expect you to play it, and no excuses will be accepted.

I am reminded of the story of the cricket statistician who earned a reasonable living from reporting club cricket for the local paper and compiling the official statistics for all the teams in the neighbourhood. He was a popular speaker at cricket dinners and, after a few years of settling into a very pleasant groove, he felt confident that he would never be asked to do the one thing that terrified him — take part in a cricket match. All might possibly have been well had he not got married.

(As a lengthy aside, I would like to point out that although I am serving up as Awful Warnings the cases of two men whose downfall can be traced to their decision to get married, I have nothing against the state of matrimony, nor against the sex with whom it is most usual for men to combine in holy wedlock, viz. women. The conclusion that should be drawn from these parables is not that marriage should be avoided, but that cricket bats and coaching manuals — notably this one — should be taken on honeymoon, because the one inevitable consequence of marriage in England is a game of cricket.)

As is quite common in married life, after a while children started appearing, at least until the happy couple found out what was causing it. The proliferation of nappies and bottles did not hinder our hero's progress in his statistical career, but suddenly one day, when his eldest son was eleven years old, the day of reckoning arrived. It was a Wednesday afternoon and there was no cricket being played locally, so, as he often did, our numerate friend went to collect his son from school. At the school gates he was accosted by the games teacher.

'Are you Jimmy's father?' asked the games teacher.

'Yes,' said Dad, wondering what offence his high-spirited son had committed on this occasion.

'We know you are such an expert on cricket, and we wondered whether you are free on Friday week.'

'Yes,' replied Dad, falling feet and all to his doom. 'Would you like me to talk to the boys about cricket? I'd be delighted.'

'No, it's not that,' replied the games teacher. 'It's the Fathers

Cricket Match, and it's very kind of you to agree to play.' With that he turned on his heel and, showing the sort of pace you would expect from a professional sportsman, was gone. Jimmy's Dad was left alone and palely loitering.

Friday week came all too quickly. The sun shone brightly in an unbroken blue sky, and Jimmy's Dad made his way to school with more reluctance than ever he did during his days as a pupil there. When he finally arrived, he was greeted with another slap with a wet sock.

'You'll captain, won't you?" said the games teacher.

Too weak to argue, Jimmy's Dad nodded his head listlessly and went out to toss up with the School 1st XI captain, who was no taller than four foot nine. The toss was quickly lost, and the Fathers were invited to bat.

In retrospect, it was not so much the playing that blighted a life that hitherto had enjoyed all things connected with cricket. It was the great expectations of the parents and the boys in the crowd that caused the disaster.

'Your Dad's really ace at cricket, isn't he, Jimmy,' was the gist of the boyish chatter around the boundary, while the parents looked across at the captain of their side and expressed the hope that he would show some mercy on the boys on the way to his inevitable triumph. Jimmy's Dad sat ashen-faced awaiting his turn to bat.

He had put himself down at number eight, and prayed that his first seven batsmen would score enough to enable him to declare before his services would be required. Unfortunately they did not. At 102 for 6, he walked nervously out to bat, debating with himself as he did so whether to take guard right or left handed. In the event he chose to play left handed, a decision that may well have been wrong.

The first ball, from an eleven-year-old bowling gentle right-arm over, was straight if nothing else, and the captain played down the wrong line. The bails toppled quietly to the ground, and with them went Jimmy's Dad's reputation as a cricketer. The rest of the day was a black haze of incompetence, resulting in the first victory by the Boys for seventeen years. And all because one man

'... the captain played down the wrong line...'

thought that playing cricket was something that would never happen to him.

I am pleased to be able to report a far happier final outcome to this particular affair than in the case of Ricardo Romero. After two or three months of deep depression, suicide attempts and failure to mow the lawns on alternate Friday evenings, Jimmy's Dad sent off for a Primary Club tie, which he then wore on every occasion connected with his son's school.

'Oh, this tie,' went his well-rehearsed reply to the polite enquiries. 'It's a Primary Club tie — you know the charitable club you can only belong to if you've ever been out first ball in a cricket match. Managed to organise my qualification, if you know what I mean, playing for the parents here last summer.' Suddenly his total failure as a cricketer and a parent was turned into a charitable action, with the added implication that never before had he been out first ball. His image as a fine cricketer and a gentleman was restored.

If cricket is to be played, it is best that it is played successfully. As a result of some minor oversight on the part of the Almighty, not all of us were born to be super-athletes, and some of us have been dished out astonishingly meagre natural resources upon which to draw in time of cricketing need. But if natural ability is all that makes a cricketer, then why do most of us bother? What Jimmy's Dad discovered, and what Señor Romero never knew, is that success in cricket can be measured in so many ways that all you have to do is to discover the right yardstick for your performance and success will automatically follow.

The odd thing about cricket is that many of the people who play it regularly, devotedly and on purpose are entirely devoid of talent for the game. This does not happen in any other sport. People who are no good at other things give up, but not the cricketer. It is not, therefore, only those who find themselves unavoidably roped in for one game of cricket per decade who need to learn how to maximise their potential on the cricket field. There is a far larger market among those regular club and village cricketers, yes and Test cricketers too, for whom success is a score in double figures or a bowling analysis of 1 for 40, and for whom the ultimate failure is the prospect of not being asked again to play. These people are fanatical about their cricket, and it is at them that this book is directed — with, I hope, more accuracy than my away-swinger which once caused the square-leg umpire to call for a helmet.

*　　*　　*

When I was a boy, it was the 1954 Pakistanis who turned me into a cricket fanatic. I was only six the previous year when the return of the Ashes crowned the many sporting achievements of that Coronation year, and the events flowed past me without ever disturbing my childish summer days. The next year was quite different. I do not know why I should have been stirred into a lifelong devotion by these strange men with strange names who splashed their way through one of the wettest summers on record. Perhaps it was the very strangeness of their names that did it. Pronouncing English names like May, Hutton and Trueman

16

presented no challenge, but words like Imtiaz Ahmed, Fazal Mahmood and Hanif Mohammad were mountains to climb for a seven-year-old with persistent tonsillitis and gaps in his teeth. A.H. Kardar was boring, because his name was too easy to remember, although he gained a little status in my eyes a year or two later when I learned of his previous incarnation as the Indian, Abdul Hafeez. I have never forgiven Oxford University for demystifying Abdul Hafeez and turning him into A.H. Kardar.

At the same time I discovered county cricket. Supporting Middlesex, the county of my birth, was ruled out by the fact that my elder brother had already co-opted them as his county, so I used the simple expedient of looking at the top of the County Championship table and supporting whoever was there. This was one of the more satisfying decisions of my youth, almost on a par with deciding to try some candyfloss at Battersea Fun Fair, as it turned out that the team on top in 1954 was Surrey, who had been there in 1952 and 1953 and were destined to stick to the top as firmly as that candyfloss stuck to my chin in 1955, 1956, 1957 and 1958 as well. I had years of unstoppable success to identify with.

Identifying with success, however, is one thing. Achieving it oneself is something rather more difficult. From the age of seven my main ambition has been to play for Surrey and England. It is only now as I approach the age when all cricketers except Wilfred Rhodes, W.G. Grace and Geoff Boycott retire that I begin to understand that possibly I will not achieve this particular ambition. I have analysed in detail the reasons why I have failed to rise as high in cricketing circles as I had hoped, and the reasons are clear. It is not my background: a schoolfriend of mine won a Blue at Oxford and played county cricket. Nor is it my ability, which I freely admit is limited. It is my lack of a proper coaching manual in those formative years.

From the age of seven onwards I read them all — epics by T.E. Bailey, K.S. Ranjitsinhji, the entire MCC Cricket Committee and even, in a last desperate effort, a book called *Cricket The Australian Way*. But they all failed to point out that strokes, grips and follows-through are minor aspects of the Compleat Cricketer. What counts is attitude. In this book, I am attempting to plug the

17

gap in cricket literature that has prevented me from following my boyhood heroes, May, Bedser, Laker, Lock and Loader, into the England team. We will be learning the lesson of Bob Willis' knees — that self-confidence can overcome physical frailty. We will discover how even the least talented can influence the play of the entire team, if not the opposition as well, and how success can be achieved without even swinging a bat in anger.

If I were being entirely honest at this stage, which I might as well be because it won't happen again between these covers, I will admit that following the advice that has been so painstakingly compiled purely for your benefit will not automatically lead to selection for Surrey and England. After all, there are only eleven men in a cricket team, and my publishers and I fervently hope that more than eleven people will buy this book. However, what I can guarantee is that if you take to heart all that is written, you will no longer be surprised or disappointed by your outward lack of recognition. Within yourself you will know you are playing to your full potential.

2
LOOKING THE PART

It has become clear to me over the years that Shakespeare's rather lengthy tragedy *Hamlet* is required reading for all Compleat Cricketers. Not only must they pore over the annotated works of Donald Bradman, Alf Gover et al in an attempt to master the intricacies of the square cut and of how to adjust the thigh pad, they should also kick off their cricketing education with a quick flick through *Hamlet*. It is not read with the purpose of knowing how to deal with one's father's ghost, should he pop up unexpectedly at second slip. It does not help much, either, in advice on how to stab people in the arras, which is difficult to do with even a polyarmoured cricket bat. But it does have one general word of advice for those who wish to make their way successfully in any endeavour for which they believe their intrinsic skills may be limited.

In Act I, Scene 3, almost before the patrons of the average provincial repertory performance have settled in their seats and stopped rustling their programmes, Polonius enters the room in which his doomed offspring Laertes and Ophelia have been chatting pleasantly about the primrose path of dalliance while Laertes waits for the 1510 ferry to France. Does Polonius join in this idle banter with his children? No, he has weightier things on his mind. He turns to Laertes who, knowing what an old bore his father can be when he gets a head of steam up, is trying desperately to take his leave. But before he can get away, he is cornered and Polonius is letting rip with a few unasked-for precepts. Laertes is rolling his eyes heavenwards and shrugging his shoulders at the ineluctability of Dad's pontifications, when suddenly, out of nowhere, Polonius lets drop a nugget of wisdom, which is as true today as ever it was four hundred years ago.

Costly thy habit as thy purse can buy,
But not express'd in fancy; rich not gaudy;
For the apparel oft proclaims the man.

In cricket it is just the same as in Denmark, and if anything more so. Charles Dickens in *Pickwick Papers* added to the Universal Truth that the right kit is most of the battle by writing, 'We know, Mr Weller — we who are men of the world — that a good uniform must work its way with women, sooner or later.' (For working your way with women, see chapter 8, Fitness and You.) I apologise, incidentally, for the overdose of apt quotations. I have just picked up a heavy book to throw at the cat which was attempting to steal a piece of cold chicken left over from lunch, and it turns out to be my *Dictionary of Quotations*, which opened, on missing the cat and striking the cold chicken, at Wm. Hazlitt (1778–1830), whose views on the right kit for cricket are happily unrecorded.

The purpose of wearing a special outfit for cricket is to give the wearer confidence. Confidence is the essence of cricket, especially for players of limited talent for whom confidence may not be only the essence but also the entirety of their cricket ability. For that confidence to be maximised, attention must be paid not only to the equipment worn on the pitch, but also in and around the pavilion before during and after the match. We shall now study all aspects of cricket kit in detail.

1) Arrival at the Ground: Kit Requirements

First impressions are lasting impressions. They can vary from love at first sight to the completely inaccurate assumption that somebody who looks powerful and athletic actually is. It is essential that you give the impression of power and athleticism to the opposition, or at least avoid giving the opposite impression too completely. The rules vary slightly according to whether or not the match is at home or away, and whether you wish to impress both the opposition and your own team-mates, or merely your own team-mates, but the broad general guidelines apply in every case. There is, it goes without saying, absolutely no point whatsoever in trying to impress the opposition without also impressing your own team. The opposition will quickly learn from the hoots of derision emanating from your changing room that your appearance probably is not an outward and visible sign of any inward and spiritual ability.

There are only two possible forms of transport by which to arrive at the ground. One is on foot, and the other is in a smart open-top sports car, or a limousine of equal social cachet. Arriving on foot is usually only sensible at home games, but anything is preferable to arriving at an away fixture in a clapped out 1964 Austin A30 or the travelling salesman's standard issue Ford Cortina. Ian Botham would have trouble looking good climbing out of one of those.

The arrival should be timed for about ten minutes before the scheduled start of the match. It is not good form to arrive after the game has started, and anyway it makes you even more conspicuous than is necessary for the correct level of confidence to be achieved. Arriving too early may give your opponents too long to look at you before the game starts, which may lead them dangerously close to drawing their own conclusions as to your abilities. The match will never start on time anyway, so arrival on foot or in an open-top BMW at 2.20 for a 2.30 start maximises your ability to make an impressive entrance.

2) From Car To Changing Room

As you step out of your car, or out of the shadows of the trees by the boundary, the opposition (those who have arrived early, not having paid attention to the previous paragraph) will have their first chance to look at you and to size you up. What will they see? Will they see a formidable athlete, or will they see an incompetent makeweight who will bat no. 11 and not get a bowl? You must ensure they see the former, because if they fail to recognise an incompetent makeweight when one emerges into the limelight his troubles are fewer. Incompetence, like beauty, is in the eye of the beholder.

Making yourself look like a formidable athlete is not achieved merely by hiding behind a life-size cardboard cutout of Johnny Weissmuller or Henry Cooper. It begins in the privacy of your bedroom at home (as do a lot of things). Look at yourself in the mirror, stare long and hard at the expanse of pasty flesh or shrunken chest that faces you and ask yourself in all honesty, Am I the Donald Bradman type, small but with lightning reflexes and wrists of steel, or am I the Clive Lloyd type, tall, lithe and panther-like, smouldering with pent-up energy? Or perhaps the Ian Botham type, large, vigorous and muscular? Even if you are a little overweight and rather flat-footed, remember Colin Cowdrey. Your session of self-analysis in front of the mirror should give you a model to build yourself upon, a formidable athlete whose basic shape resembles yours, whose outward appearance and mannerisms you can adopt to strike fear, or at least doubt, into the opposition before the game has started. The possibilities are endless. If you are small and bald, so was 'Tich' Freeman,

'... *a formidable athlete* ...'

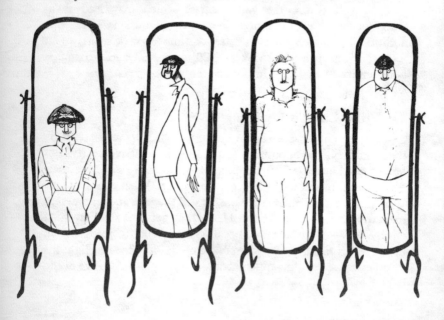

who once took 304 wickets in a season. If you are small and married with eight children, so was Bobby Abel of Surrey, who nevertheless scored 357 not out for Surrey against Somerset in 1899. If you have no kneecaps but plenty of hair, your description matches that of Denis Compton. One arm shorter than the other — you're probably another Len Hutton. Poor eyesight — think Boycott, Barlow and Bowes; drunk as a skunk — so was Robert Peel ... and so on. Whatever your shape or deformity, you are potentially a great cricketer. Fit that mould, more like the athlete you might have been if only some vestige of talent had been yours, and with luck you can fool the opposition long enough to get into the changing room without rousing suspicion.

A brief word here on the clothes you should wear to the match. The long and frank sessions of nakedness with mirrors in the bedroom will have decided for you whether you are basically an amateur (Dexter, Cowdrey, W.G. Grace etc.) or professional (Boycott, Abel, Hutton etc.). The amateur type must inevitably turn up wearing blue blazer, cravat, grey flannels and probably a motoring cap. The professional type, on the other hand, should arrive on foot wearing a leather apron, collarless shirt open at the neck and rolled to halfway up the biceps, with bicycle-clips creasing the turn-ups of the black trousers and revealing dainty black army boots. Bloodstains on the apron are an optional extra, as is a knotted handkerchief on the head.

The Kit is carried from car to pavilion either in a large leather cricket bag made in 1932 and bearing the initials W.R.H., or else in a collapsible reflective silver pouch bearing the advertising slogan of any company in no way connected with cricket — a Japanese drugs firm or a Greek shipping line, for example. Both types of receptacle are guaranteed to confuse the interested observer. A proper cricket holdall implies that the bearer is keen to be considered a cricketer, and therefore by implication is not.

3) The Cricket Bag Unpacked

If this had been written perhaps ten years ago, it would have been a very brief paragraph indeed. Contents of cricket bag — one white shirt, one jockstrap, one pair white socks, one pair boots, one pair cream flannels, one short-sleeved jersey, one long-sleeved jersey, cap, abdominal protector, bat, pads, gloves — end of para. But times have changed. Cricket equipment is big business, and the successful cricketer needs the right stuff to help him on his way.

Having established therefore that the description of the correct cricket Kit will occupy more than a couple of lines, let us subdivide the contents of our cricket bag, figuratively if not literally, into two parts, Dress and Equipment. We will then take a look first at the Dress requirements of the successful cricketer.

The obvious thing to say about cricket clothing is that it is white. For the first match of the season, the clothes must be clean. As the season progresses, your consistent but inevitable reselection for the team of your choice (see Chapter 4) will lead you to a compromise between cleanliness and divorce. The occasional green mark on the knee or elbow will inevitably remain for more than one week if the person responsible for keeping your kit clean is not always galvanised by the challenge of ironing your cricket trousers for the eleventh Monday in a row. This basic fact is understood in cricketing circles, and spotless clothing week in and week out is a sign of either an incompetent cricketer or a man still on his honeymoon. If you are the former, you would do well to add your own stains before the next match. If you are the latter, your cricketing skills will soon start to suffer, mark my words.

Cricket shirts used to be very straightforward to advise on: white, cotton or flannel. Now, however, we have shirts with short sleeves, shirts in polyester, shirts with coloured trim on collar and cuff and tunic style with tailored waists. Decisions are needed. The good news, however, is that the old-style white cotton shirt is still the best. The Test teams these days look rather weedy in their short-sleeved shirts. Those of us for whom the ultimate in aggressive commitment to cricket was Fred Trueman at the moment of delivery, hair flying, shirt sleeves and tails flapping in the breeze, will never be able to reconcile ourselves to tunic-style tailored waists. It is not necessary either. A shirt is a shirt is a shirt. Most cricketers do not anyway have particularly well-tailored waists, which makes shirts of that ilk an optional extra that should not be opted for. An XL white shirt is all that is needed. I favour my grandfather's dress shirt, which is so large it took three Lancashire cotton mills two weeks to produce. This shirt will pass down the generations, breathing hostility at opening batsmen for years to come, whether or not the wearer of the shirt is actually opening the bowling. It is the one item of Kit that always passes the pre-season inspection as I would need to put on at least 15 stone over the winter before there is any pressure on any of the buttons. At that weight I would be more likely to be selected as the heavy roller than opening bowler.

The pre-season kit inspection, as well as a routine pre-match inspection, is crucial, and with no garment more so than the cricket flannels. Trousers have a strange knack of shrinking during the winter months, and many is the unsuspecting cricketer who has arrived at the ground for the first match of the season with a pair of flannels barely big enough to fit his eleven-year-old son. What makes matters worse is that it is not only flannel that shrivels in the cold. The new man-made fibres shrink just as badly stuffed away in a drawer or on a hanger for the winter months. Polyester/viscose material with side adjusters will not help solve this great mystery. Frankly, I take a traditionalist view on trousers as well. Ever since Gary Sobers loped onto the pitch wearing bell-bottomed flannels in the mid-sixties, there has been an influential school of thought that decrees that cricket trousers should be as fashionable as Seve Ballesteros' golfing trousers or Gussie Moran's frilly knickers on the Centre Court at Wimbledon. I am hardly one to argue with Sir Garfield on matters cricketing, but I doubt whether he has had the hands-on experience of successful village cricket trousers that I have. In any match below professional level, who is the man to watch? Is it the twenty-year-old with the complete brand new outfit bearing the names and logos of the most fashionable sports outfitters of the day? No, it most certainly is not. The danger man is the chap in the faded yellow flannels (with turn-ups and fly buttons), who probably inherited his cricket equipment from his grandfather. The point is that his grandfather quite likely played county

'... a variety of aromas...'

cricket in his day, and grandson has probably inherited much of his talent along with his trousers. Elderly cricket garb is a sign of inherited skills, and therefore it is well worth having an item or two of pre-war vintage in your bag. It keeps the opposition in a state of mild concern, which with the aid of large slices of luck can be transformed into despair as the day wears on.

The place to buy your trousers, then, is not the local sports shop (10% off for members of the local club) nor even from the glossy mail-order advertisements in the sports magazines. Buy them at the local parish jumble sale. For pure strategic value, they will be well worth 50p of anybody's money. While you are there, look around for socks. Standard white tennis socks may only cost a couple of pounds new, but two pairs of well-used grey (Bob Willis' recommended colour) woollen socks at 10p each will probably ward off blisters and opponents alike more effectively than any fresh-smelling brand new pair of white polyester/nylon ones. Socks are one item that must without fail see the inside of a washing machine on a weekly basis. In my early youth I played for a team of mostly unmarried men. With nobody to do our washing for us we gave off a variety of aromas which were mutually exclusive. By the third or fourth game of the season it was impossible to persuade anybody to stand at second and third slip at the Ploughman's Arms end, as the combined effect of the wicket-keeper's and long leg's socks, borne unerringly slipwards by the prevailing winds, made mustard gas in the trenches of Ypres seem positively bracing in comparison. The opposition were thus able to cut everything towards third man, which was a position rarely filled as it meant placing a man by the pavilion and thus polluting the air the spectators were trying to breathe. Clean socks are a basic requirement of the cricketer, at whatever level of achievement.

The colourful bits of a cricketer's wardrobe are the sweaters and the cap. The English summer being what it is (i.e. cold, wet, windy), you will obviously need at least one each of the long and short sleeved varieties of sweater. As an aside, I could here refer to thermal underwear, string vests and wet suits which can provide extra warmth in sub-Arctic conditions, but any simple manual about climbing the North Face of the Eiger in January at night can give you similar information, so I will not waste further space here.

The cricket sweater must be colourful. It must also be old and baggy. The best cricket sweater of all is unquestionably the MCC sweater. Apart from the potential for dazzling opposition batsmen with the glare of the carrots and custard colours, the value of an MCC jersey in runs to your side cannot be underestimated. No batsmen will take a quick single to the man patrolling the covers in MCC colours, provided you can at least convey an image of panther-like agility for an over or two. Pulling the MCC-coloured wool over your own eyes may with luck also pull it over the batsman's.

Cricket caps are another matter. These come in hundreds of

colours, designs and shapes and have now been largely superseded by the sunhat (white) and the helmet (see p. 30). Caps gave
colour to the game and could often in the home counties be used
by low-flying jets as beacons to bounce their radar off as they
turned for their final approach to Heathrow. It must surely only
be a matter of time before the sports outfitters start producing
sunhats in club colours, to replace the technologically outmoded
cap. In the meantime, avoid caps unless the entire team wears the
same one which can be very intimidating, like playing against the
chorus line from *The Student Prince*. Wear the white sunhats,
which are no less useful in the absence of any sun in England than
a cricket bat in the absence of any ability to wield it. Cricketers
wear sunhats, so you should wear one.

I will now deliberately avoid devoting a paragraph to the
athletic support. Buying the item is embarrassing enough for the
average Compleat Cricketer, who is, as you will by now appreciate, a delicate flower. Writing about the thing is even worse. I will
only say that if you do summon up the courage actually to ask for
one in a shop (bearing in mind that the intimate goods depart-
ments in sports outfitters are staffed entirely by women) always
ask for the XL size. The size refers to the dimensions of your
waist rather than of any part of the anatomy that might be
athletically supported, so you will certainly need the XL size (at
least until you have read Chapter 8). What's more, the ladies
behind the counter serving you are not, or should not be,
purchasers or wearers of said article, and thus might in their
ignorance be impressed by any man who needs an XL jockstrap.

On the borderline between Dress and Equipment come the
boots. To be more precise, one can define cricket shoes as dress,
but cricket boots are really pieces of equipment, offensive
weapons rather than armour for the knights of the cricket field.
Cricket shoes of yore were brown and worn by the Under-Eleven
XI at my prep school. Once you reached your eleventh birthday
or your feet hit size three, whichever was the sooner, boots took
over from shoes in the junior cricket bag, never to be superseded.
Boots encased the feet of Jack Hobbs during every one of his
61,237 runs, and even the delicate footwork of a Frank Woolley

or a Donald Bradman was accentuated by the heavy white framework of their cricket boots. So all cricketers, from the MCC to the High Dudgeon Sunday XI, wore cricket boots. Nobody wore shoes.

Nowadays, foot technology has moved on. Cricketers can wear boots (with optional screw-in studs and/or drag-plate and toe cap) or shoes, many of which are made in Germany or Taiwan or other such bastions of cricket culture. I have to admit I don't recommend shoes. In my first (and to date only) game wearing cricket shoes since my eleventh birthday, I played over a yorker which landed with remarkable accuracy on the instep of my back foot. I was given not out to the lbw appeal which ensued, but I would have preferred that insult to the injury actually sustained. I have never been noted for the technical merit or artistic skills of my hopping, but in this instance I moved rapidly and athletically on my one surviving leg away from the scene of the crime. Had I been wearing my cricket boots, this would never have happened. The ball would probably have bounced harmlessly off my boot and into the wicket-keeper's teeth, and the resulting confusion would probably have been worth two leg-byes, which by dint of judicious discussion with the scorer at a later date could have been converted to two runs onto my total, a significant boost to the annual run tally. Boots, not shoes, must be worn.

We now move on to the technologically mystifying subject of Cricket Equipment. It was not so long ago that cricketers batted in Test Matches without even the benefit of batting gloves. Just two pads and a bat was all they needed to score a double hundred before tea. But of course, time waits for no man, and with the passing of time things can only get progressively more marvellous. A batsman these days (whether no. 1 for England or no. 8 for Lower Scoring Sunday Team) will wear, as a minimum, from top to bottom:

1) Helmet;
2) Chest Pad;
3) Fore-arm Protector;
4) Batting Gloves;

5) Abdominal Protector;
6) Thigh Pad;
7) Leg Guards;
8) A Bat.

He will then score 7 in an hour and a half against the leg-spinners. Where would we be without the white heat of the technological revolution, as applied to cricket? The truth of the matter is that while items 4 to 8 inclusive are of real practical value, items 1 to 3 serve a vital psychological purpose. Let us consider them each one in turn.

The helmet has revolutionised cricket. Any batsman who perhaps in his darkest moments had to admit that Dennis Lillee can be a little frightening to face up to can now smile confidently as the fastest of opening bowlers steams in towards him sure in the knowledge that any bouncer will smash into his helmet, causing only a slight concussion, or else whizz past his left ear and knock the wicket-keeper out. Helmets have two further very significant advantages over the common or garden cricket cap, which even for those cricketers who do not regularly have to try to take the shine off the ball at Sydney or Lahore are well worth bearing in mind. Firstly, they imply a certain level of batting ability. Would anybody whose highest score ever is 14 and who boasts a career average of 2.87 bother to invest in a helmet? No. Anybody who marches out to bat in a helmet is assumed to have considered the expense worthwhile, in terms of likely hours in the firing line. It can have a very depressing effect on the fielding side for them to be forced to consider the possibility that he might be a reasonable batsman, and provided said no. 7 has learnt to take guard correctly (see Chapter 3), it may be as many as two or three balls before they realise that the helmet does not mask any great talent. By then it may be too late. A snick through the slips and his career average will have been boosted to 2.88. The investment has paid off.

The other major advantage of wearing a helmet is that it renders the batsman unrecognisable. Where once spectators and scorers alike could tell the batsmen apart by the colour of their hair or the jaunty set of their caps, now all are rendered indistinguishable underneath the blue helmet and visor. This anonymity can only help the performance of the weaker batsmen in the team. If the fielding side do not know who is facing, they cannot set the field to cut off your only stroke (a knitting needle prod through second slip). If the scorer cannot tell who hit that last four, there is at least a 50:50 chance of credit being given where credit is not due, much to the benefit of nos. 9, 10 and Jack. The helmet is clearly worth the capital outlay involved. You may be able to recoup a fraction of the cost involved by trading in your cap in part exchange.

The chest pad is of little value unless you suffer from terminal puniness and wish to appear more bulky. Certainly a chest pad will render very weedy cricketers visible from side on, provided the weight involved is not too great for their spindly frames. Perhaps the best answer is to wear your chest pad under a Superman T-shirt, so that the Superman logo is just visible at the open neck of your white shirt. The opposition will worry about whether or not you are Clark Kent in disguise, until they realise that Superman is from Krypton, which is not yet a member of the ICC. A very rich cricketer of my acquaintance used his wallet stuffed in his breast pocket as a chest pad, but this did him no good. He was regularly run out, slowed by the weight of well-thumbed tenners that he liked to keep on his person. The one time his wallet took a direct hit, he suffered severe lacerations to his rib cage caused by the splintered plastic of his credit cards. Thereafter he left his money at home, which not only improved his batting but also gave him a perfect excuse for not buying any drinks in the pub at the end of the day.

Fore-arm protectors are fine for Geoffrey Boycott going out to face Marshall, Holding and Roberts. At any lower and slower level they are only of value when a batsman is terrified of the opposing fast bowlers, i.e. in almost every game played on every village green on every Sunday. At High Dudgeon, we often use the fore-arm protector as it takes the opposition an extra over to work out whether the wearer is a class batsman nursing an old injury, or an incompetent coward who is trying to bluff them.

At the end of the fore-arm we find the hand, if I remember my Negro Spirituals correctly ('arm bone connected to de hand bone, hand bone connected to de finger bone' etc. etc.). On the hands, batting gloves are worn. When I was a young lad playing for the School Under-Eleven XI, batting gloves were simple affairs of cotton with spiky green rubber strips on the back of the hand as protection. These were adequate against the speed of the next door school's Under-Eleven XI's opening attack, and they had the bonus of being perfectly designed to inflict maximum damage to the wicket-keeper and close fielders if it was felt that they deserved a thump. Under-eleven-year-olds often deserve a thump.

That style of glove is now as outmoded as are the brown cricket shoes that I also wore when short of puberty. Nowadays gloves are described as sausages (not to be confused with sausages that taste like gloves: see Chapter 8), or else they are one-piece boxing-type mittens, which curiously cannot deliver quite such a devastating upper cut as the old green spiky ones used to do. Still, finger protection is the name of the game and there is no doubt that in this area of kit technology time has meant improvement as well as change. All new gloves are better than any old glove. The only problem is that all gloves in any club kit bag are inevitably old. They are usually also inevitably all for the left hand, except for one right hand glove for a left-handed batsman, which anyway is sweaty and smelly having just been discarded by your team's David Gower clone who was out three minutes ago, run out by his partner for 49. Glove selection can be difficult.

There are two solutions, one cheap and one expensive. The expensive answer is to buy your own pair. The cheap answer is to raid the club kit bag at the start of the match and pull out a decent pair of gloves. These are then hidden in your own 1932 leather W.R.H. kit bag until needed. Those who suggest that cricket is a team game, all for one and one for all and other such mumbo-jumbo, do not understand the importance of a clean matching pair of batting gloves to the run-making capabilities of the lower half of the Sunday batting order.

As we continue our ramble down the anatomy, we cannot skirt

round the abdominal protector, known in polite circles as the box. There are two rules regarding this item which are ignored only at your own risk.

1) You need a box.
2) You need your own box.

Using the club box is an unnecessary risk, as you do know where it has been. There is such a thing as taking team spirit too far.

Batting without a box is cheaper than vasectomy, but unless you are certain that you have done enough for the population of the world already it is more sensible to go out and buy one. This operation can be almost as embarrassing as buying the athletic support in which the box will nestle. One member of our team slipped inconspicuously into his local sports shop, noticed a protector on a shelf, picked it up and marched quickly over to the girl behind the till. With a brief mumble of 'I'll take this one', he handed over his £1.99 and was out in the open air again before a further word could be said.

That afternoon our hero pushed the newly-purchased item into place, only to discover that it was not really big enough for the job it was meant to do. This was not readily explicable as even this poor man's wife would not have described him as over-endowed, so he went out to bat in his rather confined state. The innings was described by all who saw it as brief, hectic and ultimately painful as he flailed at the first ball (a long hop down the legside) and hit it past mid-wicket with a twisting movement that wrung from his lips a high-pitched yelp. He seemed curiously reluctant to run, but as his partner was half-way down the wicket already he realised the need to head for the other end. Witnesses at the scene still talk of his curious mincing gait, the tightly compressed lips and his strangled cries as he set off on a run he was destined never to complete. After only ten yards he collapsed in an agonised heap and was run out by a distance. He was carried back to the pavilion where his wife was called upon to remove the offending article from the area of maximum pain. This she did with, it is reported, a flourish that might have been interpreted as showing little respect for the wounded man. Then all was revealed. The box

('Made with care in India') was labelled 'Boys size Age 10 to 12'.

The next Monday the wretched man had to go back to the sports shop to exchange the box for a larger one. The details of that particular encounter are unrecorded, but I hope for his sake the shop girl did not notice the bloodstains on the item he was returning. The cost of a box may seem high in terms of runs per ball received, but in terms of runs per ball retained it is clearly a bargain.

Thigh pads are useful. I use a hip flask filled with brandy, stuffed into my left trouser pocket. It works fine if a little noisily if ever it suffers a direct hit, and if I am hit elsewhere the contents can be used for medicinal purposes. I rate this item second only to the abdominal protector in terms of usefulness to the man at the crease. It can also be more effective than a third jersey in keeping out the bracing May winds.

Pads are called leg guards these days. Don't ask me why. They are also made out of a wide variety of materials for lightweight super protection and the benefit of the marketing men. The ones in the team kit bag are still the same old tatty ones they always were, with two out of three buckles per pad missing in action and the only working buckle, the ankle strap, being suitable only for an elephant wearing six pairs of socks, with the result that the whole pad dangles helplessly around the firm, slim and sinewy ankles of the average middle-order man.

The final part of the Kit is the bat itself. In my youth, bats were made of willow, required oil and were autographed by anybody who had retired at least thirty years earlier. Mine was a Bertie Oldfield bat. My brothers used equipment bearing the signatures of Frank Woolley and Patsy Hendren respectively. Times have now changed. My elder son uses a David Gower bat, while his colleagues at school use bats with holes in the back, no shoulders and coated in Supercover, Polyplastic and aluminium foil, but the run-scoring powers of all these bats seem still to depend on the user.

A good bat really only needs one outward sign — a few solid red marks on the meat of the bat. This gives the impression that the wielder of this particular piece of willow regularly hits the ball, and that the ball goes where he wants it to go, even if the actual reason for the red marks is that the bat is most effectively employed in killing moles on the lawn. One chap I used to play with (until he got the club president's daughter pregnant) listed his scores in ballpoint pen on the back of his bat, to intimidate the wicket-keeper and slips. Needless to say there was a certain amount of poetic licence in the scores recorded, but whenever he was out for a duck it gave him a chance to say, 'First one this season', in such a manner that people half believed him.

I believe in a heavy bat, as those cause more damage to forward short leg when you accidentally let go of the thing while hooking. I also tend to favour the old faithful image, for the same reasons that baggy yellow flannels can be effective. This does not mean a W.G. Grace autograph. These days a Tom Graveney or Norman O'Neill autograph is about the correct vintage. A bit of white strapping round the meat is a good idea as well–the red marks show up more effectively than on willow and linseed oil.

The kit bag is now unpacked and we are ready for the game itself. But before we step out on to the field of play, one more word of warning. Make sure your kit bag, whether very old or very new, has a locking device. I'm not worried about the security, money, watches, car keys etc., for cricketers are not dishonest. The problem is that cricketers are borrowers and bats, pads, caps and hip-flasks can become more borrowed than *Lady Chatterley's Lover* at the local public library if you are not security conscious. Your kit bag, if stocked according to the precepts laid down in this chapter, will be irresistible to all your fellows, so either lock it, or hide everything underneath your box, which is something that not even gloved hands will wish to rummage past. And so to the game itself.

3
BATTING, BOWLING AND STANDING STILL

This is getting exciting. You have the kit, you understand the socio-political significance of what you are about to indulge in, so now you are ready to learn how to play the game. Let us waste no more time.

The rules of cricket are called the Laws Of Cricket, for reasons that are unexplained, to me at least, to this day. Maybe cricket was invented by a judge. They are to be found in full in any edition of Wisden, and need not concern us here. All you need to know is that the bowler bowls, the batsman tries to hit the ball and, if he succeeds, the fielder tries to stop the ball before too much damage is done to his team's cause. From this brief but thorough statement of the workings of cricket, it can be seen that the game, like Caesar's Gaul, is divided into three parts, viz Batting, Bowling and Fielding. (The three parts into which Gaul was divided had different names, which temporarily escape me.)

How To Bat

Batsmanship is something which has no value except within the context of the match. There is no point in looking good in the nets if you are to fail out there in the middle. There is no merit in possessing a cover drive reminiscent of Hammond at his peak if, when executed, it always directs the ball straight to extra cover's right hand. What we want is runs.

It is no contradiction to say that style brings runs. Style is relaxation, and relaxation is domination of the bowling. No innings starts with the first ball. It starts some time before that with hours of dedicated posing in front of the hall mirror. It starts in the mind of the batsman as he prepares himself for the bowlers he must face. It starts very often with a ten-minute retreat to the little cubicle at the back of the pavilion.

A cricket coaching book that I was given for Christmas in 1961 includes a complete chapter by Colin McDonald, the Australian opening batsman, entitled 'When To Go In'. One might have thought that the answer does not require a full chapter, e.g. 'When the chap before you is out', but it turns out that Mr

'. . . no innings starts with the first ball . . .'

McDonald was describing the different styles and techniques required of a no. 5 as opposed to a no. 3. In first-class cricket, to which I was still aspiring in 1961, the subject is clearly worth a chapter. For the Compleat Cricketer, the question is more rapidly answered. It is no. 7.

No. 7 is the perfect position because it is virtually devoid of responsibility. If the first six score 50 apiece, then whether no. 7 fails or not is immaterial. If the score is 22 for 5 as he sets out on his innings, then for him to fail will not be unexpected, and responsibility for the defeat cannot be placed at his door. No. 11 on the other hand may be a totally incompetent batsman, but he will regularly find that he has either to attempt to hit the winning hit or else survive three overs for the draw, and if he fails the loss is his fault. He will be up against the opening bowlers brought back for the kill, and life at the wicket will be entirely unpleasant. No. 7 comes in to bat when the opening bowlers will be taking a break between their two devastating spells of the afternoon, and the bowling being dished up will be from the optimistic leg-spinners or the utility medium-pacers, who are not often the most deadly of opponents. The only problem about batting no. 7 is that there are ten other players in your team who are also jockeying for that slot in the batting order.

Once you have put on your kit and are waiting for the fifth wicket to fall, it is essential that the correct preparation, both mental and physical, is achieved. One of the events that even the most unobservant will see round the boundary of any cricket match is the next man in facing a few gentle balls from a team-mate. This is a good thing and should be part of any batsman's acclimatisation process. It actually is unlikely to do your batting any good whatsoever, but it will incidentally serve to impress your captain that you are a keen member of the side and worthy of a regular place in the XI. The main advantage of this particular piece of cricket theatre is that it serves to tire out the luckless chap who has volunteered to bowl at you, and this may well reduce his chances of doing better than you in the game at hand. Thus your attempts to climb slightly higher in the averages are rewarded.

Having someone bowl at you will also help you get accustomed to the light. Donald Bradman used to do this by walking very slowly out to bat, so you might as well throw that into the repertoire as well. If a slow walk worked for him, it cannot possibly do you any harm. On your slow way out to the crease, you will no doubt pass the outgoing batsman walking grimly back to the pavilion in the knowledge that his double century will have to wait for another day. He will inevitably mutter some advice to you as you go by. Pay no attention to him. If he really knows all the answers, how come he's out?

On arrival at the wicket, the first thing to do is to take guard. Taking guard shows the style of the man who has arrived at the crease and can influence the way the fielding side approaches the task of getting him out. Is he easy meat or will containment be the best they can hope for? The obvious guard to take is middle and leg, because most people do. The correct way to ask for this guard is to call 'Two legs' or 'Two' as opposed to 'One' when you want

'... the style of the man...'

leg-stump guard. I have never heard anybody ask for 'Three' for middle stump, but I might try it myself one day. Logic leads me to assume that off-stump guard would be 'Five Legs', which sounds more like a crippled bluebottle than a cricketing term. I do not recommend asking for such a guard.

Once your bat is in the right place, dig your crease and take a look about you. If the wicket-keeper is not standing up at the stumps, it looks thoroughly professional to dig in three or four inches out of the crease. Mark your guard with a diagonal line made with your right boot (left boot for left-footed players) from the popping crease out towards leg slip. It is not compulsory to carve a line all the way to leg slip, but if you do you might as well kick the fellow when you get there. Every little bit helps.

Guard having been taken, and a crease dug that would have passed for a trench if the match was being played at the Somme, take a moment to look about you at the field placings. This is of course a purely academic exercise as it is a gifted player indeed who can direct his shots deliberately to somewhere where no fielder lies in wait, but it is all part of the intellectual warfare that

'. . . a crease dug that would have passed for a trench . . .'

is being waged out there on the square. You are now ready to receive your first ball, which brings us on to stage two in the batsman's life, Building an Innings.

Building an Innings, in the Compleat Cricketer's dictionary, equates with surviving more than one ball. This is most easily achieved if the first ball is not straight. There are, however, ways of increasing the likelihood that the direction will be on the wayward side of wide, without needing to ask your partner to trip the bowler in his delivery stride. The simplest thing to do is to step back just as the bowler's arm is coming over to bowl. This will at the very least sow seeds of doubt in his mind as to whether or not you will do it again next ball, which will affect his confidence, and with luck he might pull a muscle or snap a hamstring as his rhythm is shattered at the climactic moment. Stepping back is unfortunately only allowed for a good reason. Otherwise it could conceivably be subject to an appeal for 'Obstructed The Field', which would be good for a paragraph in the local paper, but bad for your average. After all, Obstructed The Field is out. Good reasons for stepping back include:

1) Movement behind the bowler's arm.
2) A desire to have the sightscreen moved.
3) A sudden attack by gnats.

Of the three reasons, number one is the most frequently used, but only works when there actually is somebody moving in the incriminating area. You could of course ask your Personal Spectator (see Chapter 7) to fulfil this role, but this requires a knowledge of cricket that will often be lacking in people who actually volunteer to watch you play, so give this one a miss. Excuse number two is no good because you should have thought of it before the bowler began his run-up. However, if you want to ask the fielding side to move the sightscreen at any reasonable time, this is worth doing. Sometimes a careless rupture can result.

So this leaves excuse number three, the gnat attack. This excuse works every time provided you wave your hand airily at the imagined insects as you step back. The disruption of the

Simulated Route of Gnat

'. . . worth at least four runs an innings. . .'

bowler's rhythm is worth at least four runs an innings, which is like manna from heaven after the famine that most of us suffer for most of the summer.

You cannot, however, step back every time the bowler runs up. The game would never get finished, and there is after all a pub waiting with open arms when the afternoon's activities are over. So shape up to receive the first ball, which, if your gnat-waving efforts have been effective, will not be straight. A ball that is not on the wicket gives you the opportunity to display the one shot every batsman must have in his repertoire, the shot that you have seen every Test cricketer play only too often. This is the off-side dangle. The instructions are simple.

1)   Place front foot further forward and more to the off than it was originally.

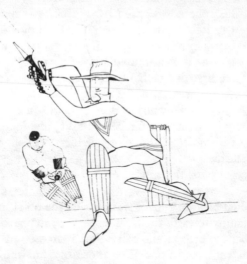

'... *the one shot every batsman must have in his repertoire*...'

2)   Lift bat, unless like Tony Greig or Graham Gooch you have lifted it already.

3)   Lean forward onto front foot, bending the knee slightly.

4)   Bring bat forward over the back shoulder until it points at extra cover. This manoeuvre is similar to that of a fly fisherman casting his line on a quiet reach of the Thames near Wallingford.

5)   By the time you have got to step 4, the ball will long since have gone past and will now be resting in the wicket-keeper's gloves (or, possibly, bouncing off second slip's shin in the general direction of fine leg). This means that there is no possibility that you will actually hit the ball, so you will not be caught. This is the whole point of the shot. It looks wonderful, promises everything, and achieves absolutely nothing except survival. I use it all the time.

Cricket teams, or at least the really great sides, consist of eleven men with but a single thought, viz. how do I get to the top of the averages? One way of doing this is by brilliant running between the wickets, of such quality that you can run your partner out without it ever appearing to be your fault. My greatest achievement in this sphere was when batting no. 7 (where else?) and I strode out to join our no. 2, who was then on 84 not out. The previous batsman had been out off the last ball of the over, so I was not called on to face immediately. Our no. 2 hit two fours and a six off the first five balls of the over and then called me for a mid-wicket conference.

'Who's that cracking girl in the bikini at square leg?' he asked.

'Their wicket-keeper's fiancée,' I said, just loud enough to be clearly overheard by the close fielders. Their wicket-keeper looked startled.

'Be looking for the single, then,' said our no. 2 as he turned back to his crease.

The final ball of the over was outside the off stump, and it was cut brilliantly towards the boundary. We ran one, and then as the fielder bent to pick up the ball before it crossed the rope, I called 'Yes' for the second one. For those of you who are not great mathematicians, I should explain that his activities in this latest over had brought our opener's score up to 98. The single made it 99, and he knew it: he always kept his score in his head. My call immediately cast doubts in his mind. His team spirit urged him to stay where he was, on 99, and take strike next over. His personal gratification pleaded for the second run, and after all, I was the no. 7. I ought to be able to survive a few balls of the next over. So he ran. Unfortunately, the hesitation before the second run, coupled with the wicket-keeper's natural eagerness to do nasty things to any man who cast a lecherous eye over his scantily-clad beloved, was enough to run him out by the narrowest of margins, for 99. My heart bled for him as he walked back to the pavilion, but I soon wiped out such sentimental feelings with a quick recital of the Compleat Cricketer's credo, 'Side Before Self'. I finished up with 4 not out that day, which gave me some small satisfaction even though we lost the match.

There are three batsmen in the history of first-class cricket in England who have finished the season averaging over 100 with the bat. They are Sir Donald Bradman, Geoffrey Boycott and Bill Johnston. The first two, we all know, are people who are actually good at batting, which is asking rather too much of my readers to emulate. But the third man, W.A. Johnston of Victoria and Australia, had a style much closer to our hearts. In 1953, this fellow came to England, ostensibly as a fast left-arm bowler, and spent the summer compiling 102 runs. He was neither a great stylist nor even a particularly competent batsman, but in 17 innings during that Coronation summer, he was only out once. Therein lies the secret of how to be a great batsman. Bat low down in the order, snick the odd four and don't get out. Run the other guy out, retire hurt, appeal against the light, anything — but do not get out. Then you too can be top of the averages. And that is how to bat.

How To Bowl

Bowling is fun and it really is pretty easy. You do not need any special equipment except the ball and a straight arm. Some clubs will supply a small metal or plastic disc for use as a marker for the start of the run-up, but I prefer to mark my kick-off point by scraping at the ground with my front foot like an incensed bull preparing to charge. One has to take every opportunity to add to the batsman's discomfiture. Apart from the above, all you need is yourself.

The difficulty is in persuading the captain to let you bowl. Unlike batting and fielding, bowling is one aspect of the game that not everybody needs to tangle with, and if a captain already has six bowlers in his line-up, there is often an understandable reluctance to turn to a seventh. In your first game for a team (see Chapter 4), it is a simple matter as the captain will at some stage in the afternoon turn to you and ask, 'Do you bowl?' The correct response is a modest shrug of the shoulders and the mumbled statement, 'Well, a little.' You will then be given at least six balls to show your worth, which may be five more than you will get as a batsman. If this is not your first game, and if thus your bowling prowess is well known, do not despair. You have been picked for the match despite what they know about you, so being asked to bowl is not impossible. My view is that a bowler of limited talent should adopt one of two styles, the slow optimistic leg-breaker or the fiery but erratic speed-merchant.

The slow optimistic leg-breaker, who is advised to have an even slower and more speculative googly in his armoury as well, should adopt a bowling style modelled on the action of a sub-lieutenant going over the top at Mons. The arm comes over delivering the ball in a high but deadly arc (technically described as 'giving it air'), as of a grenade minus pin. The probability is that the bowler will be hit as often and as hard as our man at Mons, but occasionally he will be lucky and account for a member of the opposition. This is called 'buying wickets' and has as its main tactical ingredient a very large slice of luck.

The slow optimistic leg-breaker can never expect recognition from above because leg-breaks are now officially deleted from the list of balls worth bowling at first-class level. The fiery but erratic speed-merchant has far greater prospects of advancement. Look how many otherwise quite incapable cricketers answering to this description have made it to county and even to Test level over the years. The technique is to come tearing in from at least a twenty-pace run-up and let the ball fly in the general direction of the batsman. From the moment it leaves the bowler, the ball's path is determined by laws of kinetic energy and chance, which often seem to put it on a collision course with second slip's teeth. The f. but e. s-m. usually ends up with a far better analysis than the s. o. l-b., simply because he is more difficult to hit. However, the batsman can expect that the off-side dangle will see him through an over or two, while byes rapidly take over as the side's top scorer. Once in a while the ball will hit either the stumps or the batsman, who will then have to walk or be carried back to the pavilion. The secret is to make this happen at least once before your run-up takes so much out of you that oxygen is required every other ball.

The decision as to whether or not your particular style of cricket is more suited to the leg-breaks or the fiery speed is best taken on a basis of physique, temperament, size of feet etc., and far be it from me to influence any of my students in this regard. However, I would be failing in my duty if I did not point out that

'... a high but deadly arc...'

'... *the fiery but erratic speed-merchant* ...'

one of the main benefits of going in for the quick stuff is that the ball needs to be shiny and new for this, and the established way of maintaining a shine after it has been carted into the field across the road a few times is by rubbing it vigorously on the inside of the upper thigh. This can create a sensation of well-being only normally associated with being in close proximity to the village constable's nineteen-year-old daughter, and is a major factor, I believe, in the rise of seam bowling throughout the land. Spin-bowlers only get to rub the ball in the dirt.

But back to basics. In bowling, the grip is of great importance. For right-handed bowlers, hold the ball in the right hand. Left-handers, hold it in the left hand. As you bowl, an operation which involves a certain amount of trial and error in the science of keeping the arm and the direction straight, concentrate most keenly on the follow-through. This is probably the single most important factor in a match-winning bowling performance.

The team-spirited Compleat Cricketer will follow through with a stud-curdling shuffle down the middle of the wicket, thus digging up a suitable rough patch on a length and in line with off stump for his partner to bowl at. However, as team spirit among Compleat Cricketers only usually flows in the Ploughman's Arms after the match, and then only in limited doses unless it is somebody else's round, make sure you do not follow through anywhere near the wicket unless a) you have money on the fellow at the other end to take more wickets than you, or b) you have negotiated with your captain to let you change ends next over.

You may feel, as you move in on your run-up which makes the Labour Party's European policy look co-ordinated, that you are unlikely ever to get anybody out. This may be true, but unlikely does not mean impossible, not in my dictionary, anyway. (In my dictionary, they are not even the same part of speech.) In an attempt to start taking those wickets that may indeed be few and far between, you must learn how to appeal. Appealing is the one part of cricket that takes practice, and my rule of thumb is that if the batsman misses the ball or hits it only part of the way to the boundary, appeal. Remember, the umpire (see Chapter 6) is also a human being (more often than not) and may well be holding a totally unjustified grudge against the batsman, who is, be it not forgotten, probably his team-mate and possibly higher in the averages. So appeal, and watch awe-struck as you win lbw decisions with balls that were hit hard to square leg, just because the batsman ate the last egg sandwich at tea.

There are a number of ways to appeal. I usually advocate the Tarzan yell, delivered as you turn round at the end of the follow-through. The decibel rating should be at Heathrow levels, and the arms should be outstretched towards the umpire, index fingers pointing at his throat. A chorus line of slips repeating in harmony the basic cry and at the same time jumping into the air with arms held high will add force to the appeal. It is a strong-hearted umpire indeed who can turn down more than three of those.

The quiet but urgent appeal is good if used sparingly. 'How *was* that?' with the accent on the second word and spoken in a

'... *the quiet but urgent appeal*...'

How *was* that?

conversational tone is very convincing. Jim Laker used to combine this with a very clever turn that left him looking at the umpire with legs crossed below the knees (Mr Laker, not the umpire). This style of appeal worked very well for him, and even in these days of covered wickets I am sure it can work for you.

The strangled half-appeal is a very powerful weapon. 'Howz —, no, sorry umpire. Pitched outside leg.' This is sheer poetry. The umpire and batsman learn that you are keen but fair, and by using that semi-appeal for a ball that would otherwise have been given as a wide, you are building a very strong case for all future full-blooded appeals, which everybody will know to be entirely devoid of gamesmanship.

Finally, there is the confidential whisper as you walk back to your mark. 'Last one was close, eh, ump!' or 'Would you have given that if I'd appealed?' Very good for getting the umpire on your side, and if the answer to the second remark is 'Yes', then appeal immediately. You will have worked hard for the decision and thoroughly deserve it.

The last, and in many ways the most time-consuming, aspect of bowling is Setting A Field. You know how long it takes England or West Indies to set their field for each over, but they work with the advantage that their bowlers will more often than not bowl it where they are aiming, and therefore there is some point in time spent moving deep fine leg two feet to his left. In your class of cricket, forget it. Make sure you have a total of eleven men on the field, and try to make sure that most of them are facing the batsman most of the time. To expect more co-operation than that is mere wishful thinking. If any of your team had baked beans for lunch, station them close in and upwind of the batsman. This is called intimidation, and intimidation and the arts of bowling have of late forged an unbreakable partnership. Let the rest of the layout of your field be the responsibility of your captain (see Chapter 5). He will take most of the credit for any successes, so let him take the blame for your failures.

Which brings us on to the third element in the trinity of cricket.

How To Field

The bowler bowls, the batsman bats and the other ten men are 'the field'. Betting men talk of 'the field' when referring to the no-hopers in the race, but it was obviously a cricketing gambler who originated the use of the word 'bar' as another way of saying the same thing. Most of the men in the cricket field are no-hopers who play to increase their familiarity with the area's public and saloon bars. This fact is crucial background information in any assessment of the fielding potential of the Compleat Cricketer.

All the same, many is the player who has been described as 'worth his place for his fielding alone'. So it is right to look at the rudiments of this activity, especially as few Compleat Cricketers are worth their place for their batting or their bowling alone. By their willingness to stay motionless but awake in the outfield for hour after hour, is it true to say that they can make themselves more desirable to a selection committee already wringing their hands in despair at the lack of locally available cricketing talent? The answer is a very positive no, unless your wife also makes good teas, but that must not discourage us from learning all there is to know about fielding.

Considerable research over the years has gone to show that most balls bowled do not require to be fielded. They either go through to the wicket-keeper or else are played gently back to the bowler or ferociously wide of any fielder. Any man who has to field more than half a dozen difficult ones per afternoon should feel hard done by. Fielding is therefore much more image than reality. Your job is to make the batsman think you are another Colin Bland, even if, truth to tell, you are just another Pigling Bland. This is how it is done.

1)   Study how Derek Randall moves in the outfield. It is really quite easy to do a passable imitation of his bending, bobbing style of moving rapidly in as the bowler bowls (cartwheels an optional extra), and this will immediately establish you as either a great fielder or a great mimic. With luck it will take the batsman all afternoon to find out which.

2) Never throw in from the outfield. Stop the ball, pick it up and threaten to throw, but don't actually let go of the ball. The throw is the biggest giveaway of the not necessarily wonderful fielder, and a bad throw encourages the batsmen rather too much. When the batsmen have stopped running, their legs turned to stone by the majesty of your Get Ready To Throw position, just lob it in underarm to the nearest fielder with an expression that clearly implies that the batsmen were lucky this time, but just wait....

3) Always back up the rest of your team's efforts. Never be the man who actually runs to stop the ball, but always be the safe pair of hands that would have picked up and thrown in with one movement, had the other fellow not cut the ball off before it reached you. This activity promotes an image of keenness and

'... Get Ready To
Throw position...'

'... a dropped catch is not good for the image...'

team-spiritedness that cannot fail to impress, at least until such time as the person you are backing up misses it. Then you are on your own.

4) Catches are the real problem. If one comes your way, you have little option but to go for it, and a dropped catch is not good for the image. The best answer is to field somewhere where catches very rarely come (i.e. first slip or deep extra cover), or else bowl a lot. Bowlers are allowed to drop catches off their own bowling as they only have themselves to blame. On the other hand, I have seen even the feeblest fielders cling on to stunning return catches just because they are desperate for a wicket. A return catch is the best publicity available, as you start to look like a good bowler and a good fielder in the same moment.

In general, fielding in the deep is more rewarding than fielding near the bat. To begin with it is far safer, and you are statistically

YOURS!

'... *crouching uncomfortably and looking very keen*...'

less likely to have to put hand to ball and thereby risk error.
Fielding at slip gives a man the opportunity to hear a few new
jokes during the course of the afternoon, but he has to spend
hours crouching uncomfortably and looking very keen. In the
outfield you can relax in the shade, chat up the female spectators
(see Chapter 7) and with luck be first into the pavilion at tea or
close of play. On some very large grounds an unfortunate deep
square leg or long-off can find himself patrolling half an acre of
pitch all on his own. In such cases it is best to get involved in
blackberry-picking or an Agatha Christie, as the game will go on
without you for hours before anybody notices. This is what they
really mean by being worth one's place in the side for 'fielding
alone'.

'... *relax in the shade*...'

4
HOW TO GET SELECTED

One of the disadvantages of cricket is that it is not a solo sport. It requires 22 like-minded people to get a proper match going. It is therefore not much good buying all the kit, practising leg glances and googlies in front of the hall mirror and declaring your availability for the next tour of Australia unless you are already a member of an XI. As an interesting side issue, we should note that in the nineteenth (XIXth) century it was apparently much easier to slip unnoticed into a cricket team than it is today because of the regular habit of playing against odds. Thus our great-grandfathers were frequently to be seen playing for or against 'XXII of the North Weald' or 'XIV of Doncaster' which meant it was obviously easier to get out onto the pitch and practise pacing the greensward than if North Weald or Doncaster had stopped selecting when they reached eleven (XI).

However there is no point in harking back to times past any more. We must adapt and make do with times present and times still to come. For this reason, I feel that a chapter on How To Get Selected will not go amiss*.

Let us assume that you have read diligently all that has gone before. You have the Kit (fore-arm protector optional), you have studied the techniques for the cover drive, the one that goes with the arm and how to take catches like the one that Benaud took in the gully at Lord's in 1956. You will now realise that there are only two things that you do not have to make your cricketing career entirely successful. One of these is a cricket team, and the other is any vestige of talent whatsoever. Do not despair! These minor shortcomings have never stopped true cricketers in the

---

* Dennis Amiss himself blew his chances of selection by touring South Africa.

past, and they need not stop us now. All you need is selection, and even a non-cricketer will tell you that selection and talent have never been interdependent. There are three simple steps to be taken towards selection, which I can now reveal.

1) Declaring Yourself Available

The first thing to realise is that it is not the team which selects you, but you who select the team you wish to play for. It is absolutely no good strolling down the High Street with a cricket bag under your arm hoping that somebody will suddenly stop and ask you if you are free for a game on Sunday. That sort of thing does not happen outside schoolboy fiction. (Actually, I wonder whether it even happens inside schoolboy fiction. Certainly Masters Bunter, Jennings and Dennis The Menace of my youth never relied on such haphazard methods of catching the selectors' eyes.) No, what you have to do is to find a selector and Declare Yourself Available. Finding a selector presupposes you have found a team for which said selector selects. Obviously the more local the team, the greater your chances of coming into contact with the relevant selector, and the greater the chances of the team being sufficiently incompetent to feel the need to embrace your talents.

Since writing those last few sentences, I have been approached by my sons, aged ten and four (X and IV) to see whether I fancy a game of French cricket in the garden. This might be construed at first glance as a perfect example of a selector approaching a player out of the blue and offering him a game, something which a few lines ago I had dismissed as being beyond the realms of schoolboy fiction. But of course it was no such thing. My sons realise that no decent game of French cricket can be played without Dad, especially if I am sitting in the corner of the garden where they wish the game to take place. So I am the selector *ipso facto*, and my sons approached me in classic style to declare themselves available for a game of French cricket which cannot take place without me. Thus it is that half an hour has passed since this chapter was begun, thirty minutes spent ferreting for tennis balls beyond the rhododendrons, arguing over the one-hand-one-bounce rule and above all Playing Cricket.

What this little event also shows is that anybody can be selected to play cricket in his own back garden. Competition is not severe, standards are low and selectors are always available for instant decisions. At the other end of the scale, getting into the England team is generally rather more difficult because competition is tough, standards are often quite high and most importantly the selectors are extremely elusive. It is very difficult to Declare Yourself Available to a fellow whose paths do not cross yours, so it is probably wiser to set your sights a little lower at first. I suggest the local village or club XI and if there is more than one team to choose from, aim for the lowest. Go into the team's local on a Saturday night and buy the players a drink. This could by the end of the evening involve you in some rather heavy expenditure as cricketers are not usually abstemious after a match, especially if they have lost. What you ought to be looking for, need I add, is a team that tends to lose more than it wins. They have more requirements for new blood, however diluted with alcohol that blood may be. Console yourself with the fact that the drinks won't cost as much as your newly acquired helmet or leg guards (see Chapter 2), and the outcome will almost certainly be a suggestion that you come along for a trial.

2) Trial By Ordeal

Trials come in all sizes. At the top end of the scale there is 'An England XI v. The Rest', in which if you are Jim Laker you take 8 for 2 and secure your future there and then. However, not all of us are Jim Lakers. A couple of notches lower down come the Pre-Season Nets. I remember watching this ritual at Fenners a few years ago when a number of undergraduate hopefuls were being put through their paces. One young gentleman, reportedly an opening batsman for his school team the season before, had obviously forgotten all that he had ever known about batting during the course of the intervening winter. There was even some doubt about whether he ought to be batting left- or right-handed.

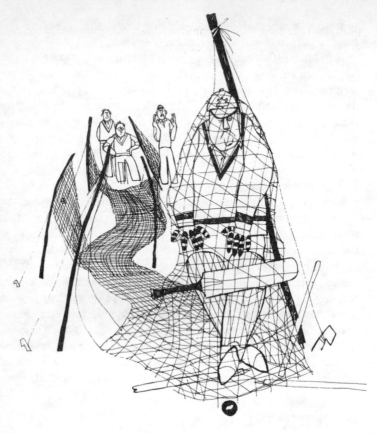

'... *it is possible that the bowlers in the nets will not always deliver half-volleys...*'

The bowlers took his wicket with diuretic regularity and a sweepstake developed over which bowler would first fail three times in a row to get him out. Each ball bowled before this event was worth 10p and a considerable sum was riding on the outcome when eventually one second-year student, a wicket-keeper by trade, completed his hat-trick of failures by bowling a slow off-break which might have had the batsman caught behind if he had been good enough to get to it. The winnings were spent in the pub, with the hapless batsman downing a double gin and tonic in compensation for failing to earn his Blue.

Trials for the average Village Cricketer are usually less nerve-wracking, although they do represent virtually your only chance of trying out those Hammond-like cover drives and that unspottable googly which have been so assiduously practised in the privacy of the home. It is possible that the bowlers at the nets will not always deliver half-volleys just outside the off stump for those strong but supple wrists you have developed to bring the bat whipping through in a perfect arc and send the ball like a leather blur along the ground to the cover boundary. It is also possible that the village no. 10 will not spot your googly but by dint of tightly-shut eyes and broad-shouldered luck will send your best deliveries back over your head at a considerable altitude. Such are the realities of cricket, which must not cause you to be disheartened.

The truth of the matter is that the very fact of securing a net with the team means that almost inevitably you will get picked for at least one game. No local selection committee is sufficiently flinty of heart to deny you at least one moment of glory. If you have the kit as well, then your longer-term status as an active member of the team is virtually assured. Nobody who brings another pair of pads to the club, another box, perhaps the very first fore-arm protector, will be spurned, at least until a more talented and equally well-equipped candidate emerges.

3)   Keeping Your Place In The Squad

Once selection has been achieved for the first time, the next goal is to keep on being selected, to retain your position in the first team squad. Of course, any club that refers to a section of its playing membership as 'the first team squad' is probably far too good for the likes of you and me, so at that stage it might be wise to go back a page or two and re-select the team you ought to be playing for. This is known as switching loyalties, and is very easy to do after the first time.

There are basically two ways of ensuring your place in the XI.

The first method is known as talent, but as this involves being good at the game there is little point in discussing it here. The other method is called Being A Valuable Member Of The Side. Value being a highly subjective commodity, one's value to the team varies according to the needs of the side. Some teams need a good opening bowler, some teams need a wicket-keeper, and some need somebody who can sell five books of raffle tickets at work and still come back for more. All teams need a player with a complete kit, or a man who can be guaranteed to buy two rounds of drinks after the game. What you must do, in the very first match you play, is to assess what the team needs and fulfil that need. It may be, for example, that nobody likes preparing the pitch before each game. Organising somebody to do a simple job like this can often engender considerable ill-feeling, so if you happen to enjoy painting the white lines for popping creases and such like, and will volunteer to do this every Saturday and/or Sunday morning before a home match, it would be very difficult for the selectors to deny your clear right to a game. Another very good ploy is to volunteer your wife, mistress, girlfriend or grandmother (but not all four) to make the teas. Provided that her sandwiches are not fatally toxic, her contribution will be wholeheartedly welcomed, not least by the other wives, mistresses, girlfriends and grandmothers who have earlier been volunteered and who have not yet found a cast-iron excuse for backing out of it. Whether your wife, mistress etc. will appreciate being made such an essential cog in the smooth-running machine that is the local XI is a different matter. You must merely remind her that great causes demand great sacrifices.

The simplest way to retain your place in the team is, however, Being Available. Availability is not as easy as it sounds, but it is the secret of being a Compleat Cricketer. Our leading players throughout cricket history have understood it. When did W.G. Grace turn down an invitation to play for England simply because he promised to visit his in-laws that weekend? Do you ever remember Don Bradman taking his summer holidays during the cricket season? Did Len Hutton ever have to do the gardening rather than play for Yorkshire? Since when did taking the

'... an essential cog in the smooth-running machine...'

children to the zoo take priority over captaining West Indies in Clive Lloyd's life? The answers are easy. Never. No. No. Never. But a little lower down the ladder of cricketing superstardom, the priorities change. Sometimes village cricketers consider clearing out the garage to be more important, at least in terms of domestic strife, than turning out for the team of a Sunday. Some cricketers even take their entire family on holiday in August, and miss as many as two consecutive weekends of cricket. This cavalier attitude to the needs of the local team must severely jeopardise the chances of the players in question retaining their places in the side, but on the positive side it gives the man who is always available a great opportunity to secure his position for once and for all. If the answer to the question 'Can you play next weekend?' is always 'Yes', then you are likely to be much higher up the list of selectees than if the answer is a monotonous 'Not next weekend, old chap,' or 'Perhaps the one after,' or (kiss of death) 'I'll ask the wife'. I should at this juncture also point out that by asking 'Can you play next weekend?' the chairman of the selectors is usually talking about availability, not intrinsic ability. He is all too well aware of whether or not you can play cricket at all, and has in his wisdom overlooked your shortcomings in that department. What he wants to know is whether you are likely to be around to be chosen for the next game. So don't say 'I still can't quite disguise my quicker one' or 'I'm not quite sure about using my feet to the leg-spinner', just say 'Yes'.

Be there. Be available. Turn up on time, wearing approximately the correct outfit, and you will be selected. You will also probably be divorced, but you can't have everything.

There is more to retaining your place in the team than just providing a willing pair of hands when the less romantic tasks associated with this wonderful game are in the offing, or even just providing any pair of hands when the total so far is less than eleven. During the match itself it is quite possible to deal a major blow to your chances of future selection, no matter how often you may have single-handedly pulled the heavy roller across the square before play began. For example, it does not do to suggest to the captain that third man should be a couple of yards finer for the left-hander. The captain has probably not even noticed that the new batsman is a left-hander, and third man is only where he is so that he can chat up the village policeman's nineteen-year-old daughter who is making the teas today. Captains do not need a clever-clogs in their team. Similarly, do not enter into correspondence through the medium of the local paper with the umpires over whether that lbw decision in last Saturday's game was justified. As you will discover in Chapter 6 (VI), the umpire's decision may be mad, wrong and even homicidal, but it is also final. Upsetting the umpires will lead you to a regular run of low scores, caught behind without getting near the shot, lbw to a ball that would have broken first slip's skull had you not got your bat in the way, or stumped off a ball that went through for four byes. If your batting is of such a calibre that you are perfectly capable of achieving low scores all by yourself without the aid of the umpires, just watch what happens to your bowling when the men in the white coats decide they wish to express their displeasure with your attitude towards them. Every wicket will be called, a little late perhaps, a no-ball. Every lbw won't be lbw, and you will suddenly discover that it is possible to overstep the crease and throw in the same action, thereby giving two no-balls to the opposition in one delivery. Your captain will be forced to take you off after but one over, if you ever manage to finish it. On the other hand, you will probably be warned at least twice during the course of the over for following through on to the wicket, so you may well be banished to long leg well before the over was due to finish. And the man who scores no runs and takes no wickets is no longer an indispensable member of the team. However many white lines you may trace before each game, such a lean spell of form must lead inexorably to the ultimate disgrace of Being Dropped. Remember, umpires are even more necessary than crease-painters.

There is one other way to lose your place in the team, and that is by being too good. This is not an eventuality that need concern many of us, and what happens in such cases is that the player drops the team rather than the team dropping the player. Just as he has earlier selected the team he wishes to play for in the first place, he now realises that his original selection was a mistake and he needs to choose another team. This is quite easy to do if you are any good at the game (so I am told). Every cricketer eventually floats up or sinks down to his natural level, and finds himself in a team where his standard of conduct both on and off the pitch is similar to that of his team-mates, and there he stays. He has selected his team, the team has selected him, and until the character of one or the other changes, there they will stay.

The team selects its opponents in just the same way. It is enjoyable playing a game of cricket on a beautiful pitch, against opposition of a similar playing standard, and halfway through the game to have a slap-up tea served by big-busted young ladies. It is no fun playing against the Gasworks XI on a pitch which doubles as the car park on weekdays, when they win by ten wickets every time and tea is a 1957 vintage rock bun dished up by the local no. 5's boyfriend. Whereas one of these fixtures will be repeated the following year, the Gasworks one will not. Over the years, a list is built up of compatible fixtures, so that even an appalling side can hope to win a game or two occasionally. If they never win a game, at least they will have been well fed at the tea interval.

Cricket being a team game, it is made up of relationships — relationships between batsman and bowler, between the home team and the visitors, between the chap at third man and the village policeman's nineteen-year-old daughter. If you are to be part of this great English institution that is Cricket, at whatever level, you must remember these relationships and fit in with them. Before a game of cricket can be played, a batsman needs a bowler, the home team needs visitors and you need to paint the white lines on the wicket. The chap at third man will have to wait until after stumps are drawn to satisfy his needs with the village policeman's nineteen-year-old daughter, but the point is well made. Cricket is a team game, and becoming part of the team is the starting point for all cricketers. Selection is all.

*　　*　　*

What if none of this works? What if you don't like marking out the popping crease? What if you can't be available next weekend? After all, you can't postpone the hernia operation for ever. What if the umpires all have plasticine effigies of you into which they stick hatpins when they wish to relieve their tensions? What do you do to get a game when all else has failed?

There are two answers, a cheap one and the deluxe version. The cheap answer is to emigrate. Give up your job, sell the house and move to somewhere where cricket is not a part of the local culture. (Can a country have culture if cricket is not a part of that culture? Are not countries lacking in cricket by definition lacking in culture? Discuss.) In such uncivilised parts of the world, your failure to achieve selection for any cricket team in England can be shrugged off as being of no importance, or else kept as a deadly secret which will keep the natives guessing and add to your mystique in your new homeland.

'Why did the Englishman leave his mother country to try to

make a living in this Godforsaken part of the globe?' I can hear the natives murmuring over their *vin de pays* or their *mai tai*, as they sit on upturned tea-chests in darkened huts, oblivious to the incessant drone of the cicadas in the undergrowth.

'I know not,' another will reply. 'Some hideous fact from his past which he wishes to keep to himself. It is connected with his hatred for white clothing and willow trees. I respect him for it.'

'Enough of this crazy Englishman,' says a third, stamping on a passing scorpion. 'Let's get back to planning next week's *coup d'état*.'

'We need the Englishman to lead us. He has no sense of fair play.'

That is the cheap alternative.

If you really want to change your way of life totally and irrevocably, choose the other option. Establish your own cricket team.

There are many precedents for this particular solution to the Unselectability problem, but all have involved a large outlay of cash. The first thing to do is comparatively money-free, however, which may be why so many people get lured into this particular means of getting a game. To start with, your team needs a name. In the early days of creating teams, the names used were logical, like Marylebone Cricket Club, if not particularly romantic. Nowadays the names are as facetious and as obscure as possible, so as to give no clue to anybody taking part that you have any deliberate connection with cricket. A name with a ring of tragedy about it is becoming commonplace. One of the most pitiful (in all senses) fixtures of the Home Counties summer is the one between the Blues and the Heartaches, two teams whose names sum up the difficulties experienced by those who attempt to run a private XI. Perhaps that shows that the team came before the name, in which case the above paragraph can be repositioned nearer the end of this dissertation.

A second, more expensive, item that a private team needs is a pitch. The alternative to this is to be a Wandering side, playing nothing but away matches, but as your opponents are more than likely to be other Wandering sides who also don't have a pitch (and who are equally desperate for a game against somebody somewhere), Wandering is fine unless you actually want to play cricket regularly. Pitches are not cheap, but a reputable estate agent can fix you up with four acres or so of suitably flat land, and after a couple of years' preparation (which includes employing a groundsman), you should be ready to go. Acquiring a pitch is a simple problem compared to the next one, acquiring a team.

Yes, there is always you to captain the side and to open both the batting and the bowling, but who will be the ten makeweights in the side? The only people likely to agree to play in the same team as Unselectable You are others who for one reason or another were spurned by their local clubs, and do you really want those sorts of people in your side? How are you ever going to find anybody who is even slightly talented, or at least knows which end of the bat to hold? These are, I am afraid, questions to which there is no answer. There are, however, one or two private wandering cricket teams surviving in Britain today, established by very rich and very incompetent cricketers, who over the course of the years have become less rich at a rate which far outstrips the rate at which they have become less incompetent. These teams inspire hope in the breast of any person with more money than sense that the establishment of one's own cricket team is possible and therefore is the solution to the predicament. A game whenever you want one, and only when you want one. Permanent selection, permanent captaincy and permanent optimism that the long overdue half-century or 5 for 5 will happen next weekend.

A man with his own team will soon learn that as long as it is his team, and exclusively his team, he will find it hard to persuade his team-mates to participate fully in the work involved in getting the team together and keeping it there. If one man is always to be captain and chairman of selectors, if that same man is always going to open the batting and run out at least three (III) of his partners per innings, then he will find that his underlings will not commit themselves fully to the greater glory of the team. If, however, he takes the democratic route and allows his colleagues a say in the selection process and opinions about the batting order and the field placings, it is inevitable that at the earliest opportunity the team will select him out. He was, after all, Unselectable before he started his own team, and there is no evidence to suggest that running one's own team makes you more attractive as a player for teams that you do not run. So the only way a man can ensure selection, even for the side he established and now runs, is to rule it absolutely but benignly. He will have to continue *ad infinitum* making all the arrangements for each game himself, acting as fixtures secretary, sole selector, baggageman, scorer, archivist and dietitian. He must become a benevolent dictator, but unlike most dictators he must not expect that his years in power will allow him to salt away a vast sum in a numbered Swiss bank account. On the contrary, the only thing that can measure the benevolence of his dictatorship is money. He must buy all the kit for his team, the scorebooks, the stumps and the white coats. He must finance the teas and the annual dinner. Bearing the cost of the annual tour to Jamaica is an optional extra, but it certainly gets players queueing up to play for the club.

Theoretically, he also needs to know a little about captaincy, but as that costs nothing he will find his team-mates always ready to give advice. He is also certain that he will remain captain as long as his funds rather than his tactics remain plentiful, so he has less need to know about running the XI on the field of play than a man who went through due democratic processes to become captain. He is the fellow who needs to read the bit on captaincy in the next chapter, not the private XI supremo. For the proprietor of a private team, that is probably the only part of this book that he does not have to read and re-read one hundred times.

5

LEADERSHIP AND VICTORY

On 21 July 1984, Lancashire played Warwickshire in the Benson and Hedges Cup Final at Lord's. Warwickshire were the pre-match favourites at 13–8 on, but Lancashire captain John Abrahams won the toss and invited Warwickshire to bat. Abrahams himself did not bowl, although he did take two important catches as Warwickshire slumped to 139 all out (Alvin Kallicharran 70). When Lancashire batted, they made a fair start against Bob Willis in his final appearance at Lord's, but Abrahams' own contribution was small (c. Humpage b. Smith 0). Thanks to a fifth-wicket partnership of 69 between Hughes and Fairbrother, Lancashire won with more than twelve overs to spare. Man of the Match, as adjudicated by England's longest-serving captain, Peter May, was John Abrahams, which made it all a very pleasant thirty-second birthday for him. It appears that leadership and victory are connected.

The status and power of a captain in cricket is far greater than in other sports. He is not just the best or longest-serving player in the XI. He is a natural leader, a man with a vision of long-term strategies and short-term tactics to win the day, a man who by personal inspiration can mould his eleven individual weak links into a chain that cannot easily be broken. Men such as this are of course readily available throughout the land, so every cricket club, from England down to High Dudgeon and all stops between, is led by such a paragon amongst cricketers.

Obviously, becoming captain is not just a matter of waiting for the position to be advertised in the Jobs Vacant column of the local paper. Unless you wish to undertake the expense of forming your own team, which as we have seen (Chapter 4) will inevitably be filled with unathletic and unsportsmanlike reprobates who could never get a game elsewhere, you will have to look deeply into your soul if you aspire to the responsibilites of captaincy. Can you read the state of the game as accurately as a Benaud or an Illingworth? Can you inspire by the brilliance of your own play like Bradman or Sobers? Can you bring out the best in your own team by superb handling of men, as Mike Brearley did? Can you pursue victory as single-mindedly as Jardine? If not, stay in the ranks. Forget about the captaincy.

The Compleat Captain has, needless to say, a far more difficult task than any mere professional captain of the 1980s, all of whom have full-time, fully paid up organisations working on their behalf. Not for Mr Gower the decision about who will mark out the pitch now that Jack or Bill or Joe has cried off at the last minute. Not for Clive Lloyd the problems of how to get to the pitch at Lower Scoring. Not for Geoff Howarth the worry about whether he should declare before tea so that he can be home in time to mow the lawn before nightfall. Little do these men realise how easy their lives are. The Compleat Captain is clearly a man among men, an inspirational leader fit to rank with Churchill, Wellington and Richard Coeur de Lion, for surely he cannot be just another put-upon muddler who somehow manages to collect eleven men together at the same time and place and keep them there until the match is over.

The main duty of the captain is to ensure that his team wins the match ahead. He may also have the longer term objective of winning match after match and therefore a trophy of some sort, but this objective often devolves into one of avoiding relegation or ignominy as the season plays out its ruthless drama. To achieve these objectives, the captain finds it necessary to indulge in a variety of short-term tactical machinations, such as winning the toss, setting the batting order, moving deep third man to silly point and putting himself on to bowl. These activities, which are of course carried out solely for the good of the team, may by chance also assist in bringing the captain a few rungs higher up the season's averages than he might otherwise have been. All responsibilities bring one or two perks in their wake.

If you go out on a winter weekend afternoon down to your local park, you will see at least three football teams engaged in an afternoon's sport about as good for body and soul as the Black Death. Teams involved in a play-off for third and fourth places in the North Broadstairs Boys Club Challenge Trophy will play as though it was the World Cup Final and a lifetime of fame and fortune depended upon every kick of the ball. Kicks of the ball, therefore, occur with rather less regularity than kicks of the opposition. The reason is simple. As Bill Shankly said with typical Scottish understatement, 'Winning isn't everything. It's the only thing.' How right he was. The vast difference between football and cricket, however, is that in football a team either wins or it does not. The eleven men usually go home either uniformly over the moon or uniformly as sick as an aviary of parrots. In cricket, it is possible to win and lose at the same time. Cricket is both an individual and a team sport, and winning does not stop at beating your opponents. If it did, this would be a very short chapter indeed. But High Dudgeon can lose by 120 runs every Saturday and Sunday for eight weeks and somebody will be able to drag victory from the wreckage. Whether it is a great catch, a spell of bowling that included no wides and only one no-ball, or something as simple as hiding the box of the man who took your regular slot at no. 7 and watching him bat like Dame Margot Fonteyn at her best, a Compleat Cricketer can find something to make his day a winning one. The man who can influence the proceedings most effectively, and therefore win most regularly, is the captain.

Act One Scene One in any cricket match is the Toss, and this is where captaincy begins. From 1952 until decimalisation in 1971, the coins of the realm had a lady on each side (the Queen and Britannia), so by calling 'The Lady' rather than 'Heads' or 'Tails' many a Compleat Captain could win the toss all season. Nowadays only the 50p coin features the two ladies, so for all but the wealthiest captains the winningest tactics this side of honesty are to borrow 2p for the toss and invite the other captain to call. You may not win the toss, but by never calling nobody can accuse you of calling wrongly. It is on little victories such as these that a

'... where captaincy begins...'

successful season is built. If you forget to give the 2p coin back to the person you borrowed it from, you will also end the season 60p or so richer than you began it.

If you win the toss, bat first. This is the advice of many a notable cricket strategist, and to follow it has the merit of not inviting criticism. The real reason for batting is however rather simpler than any knowing glances at the wicket or the sky will suggest. You bat because not all your men have turned up yet, and you can't very well ask for three or four substitutes until they condescend to reach the cricket ground. Quite probably not all of the opposition have turned up either, so let them have the shame as well as the physical disadvantage of fielding only nine or ten men, and never cease to remark on how some clubs are so badly organised that they can't even raise a team for a friendly Sunday game.

Once your team is batting, and you as captain are waiting to go in, there are a multitude of responsibilities that must be attended to. Are there two umpires? Is there a scorer? Are there enough pads to go round? Should a left-hander bat no. 4 to try to blunt the striking power of their opening bowler, a right-arm in-swing bowler? What score should we be aiming for in the first hour? How many do we need by tea-time? Has your opening bat noticed the man they've moved round to fine leg? Who's going to bowl a few at Nigel to help him get his eye in? Who will collect the tea money? The solution to all these problems is so simple it has already been widely adopted by cricket captains up and down the land. Just steal somebody's copy of the *News Of The World* and head off under a shady tree and go to sleep. You will find that the match will not stop merely because you are not watching every ball, at least not until it is your turn to go in.

When that moment arrives, when the captain of the side strides out to the wicket, the spectators cease their idle chatter and all eyes turn to the solid, reassuring figure making his way imperiously to the centre of the game. Team-mates stop biting their nails or wiping away their tears with their fore-arm protectors. Opponents see the steely determination of the man approaching the crease and realise that any further wickets in this match will have to be dearly bought. The Captain's Innings is about to take place.

All statistical surveys that I have studied have shown that the Captain's Innings is on average neither greater nor less than the innings of the other ten men, nor very different from the average innings by the same man when he is not captaining the side. In other words, the Captain's Innings is a myth. Obviously, there have been many magnificent innings by captains over the years, like Lionel Tennyson's one-handed attack of the 1921 Australians or Peter May's 285 not out against West Indies at Edgbaston in 1957, but at the same time there have been some pretty horrible failures by captains who should have known better and who I will not embarrass by naming here. Let it also not be forgotten that some of the greatest and most prolific batsmen in history were never — or hardly ever — captains, and those that were, like Hammond, Hutton, Sobers and Bradman, did not play better just because they led the side.

Frankly, this is surprising. As captain, you get the chance to bat where and when you like. You can wait till the really slow bowlers come on, or you can put yourself in before that cloud up there finally bursts and makes the pitch unbattable upon. You can appropriate the best pads and gloves, the only thigh pad and the club box to give you all the confidence you need, and you will quite probably have two team-mates umpiring who know that next week's selection depends on their ignorance of the very existence of the lbw law as applied to their leader. If under these circumstances a captain cannot make a massive score every time his turn comes to wield the willow, then he surely does not fully understand all the favourable conditions that surround his efforts.

Leadership of the batting side is not complicated. Once the batting order is decided, your players just have to go out and bat. If they are not all out by tea, then the captain can afford himself the rare luxury of deciding whether or not to declare. This decision is not based upon whether a declaration will bring the game alive and make for a thrilling two hours' worth of cricket in the evening session. It is based on two simple factors, both influenced by the convention that at tea any batting captain is expected to declare. The first factor is whether you, the captain, are not out at tea. If so, declare, as your batting average will thereby be safeguarded. This is the over-riding element in making the decision, but the second factor, i.e. whether you particularly wish to annoy the other skipper, is also worth considering. Batting on for three or four overs after tea, whether your team's score at the interval is 60 for 8 or 220 for 1, is bound to be seen as gamesmanship, time wasting, playing for the draw, tactics bordering on the unfair etc. etc. This is not surprising, because all these accusations will be true. What is satisfying to the captain batting on is the high blood pressure his decision can promote in his opponents. That in itself is worth ten runs or so.

The only thing to remember in taking the decision to bat on is to make up your mind before sitting down to tea, and to be unwavering in your determination to see it through. Then you can allow your side to tuck into all the cakes and scones they like (good for morale) while offering your opponents ever more slices of the vicar's wife's shortbread, to which there is no known antidote, in the certain knowledge that it will be the opposition who will have to be out there running around immediately afterwards, while your men have fifteen or twenty minutes to sleep it off. If public outcry from the opposition benches makes you change your decision at the last minute, then all these advantages so assiduously worked for have been thrown away.

Captaincy takes on a new dimension when you are leading the troops in the field. This is the time when all those devilish plans that you have buzzing inside your head burst out in a flurry of tactical genius that entirely confounds one side or the other. Decisions come easily to a natural leader like the typical Sunday afternoon cricket captain, and your team will follow eagerly every minor adjustment to the field, every bowling change and every word of encouragement as you lead them to yet another decisive result. Your fastest bowlers will relish bowling uphill into a Force 8 gale if you say it is for the good of the team. Fielders will be queueing up for the forward short leg spot when you put yourself on to bowl your devastating if temperamental leg-breaks. Batsmen will sink into cringeing despair when they note the precision with which you place your deep square leg a yard beyond the boundary to protect the windscreen of your new S-registered Austin Allegro.

This is the sort of leadership that can turn each weekend into an exercise of absolute power, the like of which has not been seen since the overthrow of the Russian tsars. This statement is borne out by the *nom de guerre* of the captain of a Welsh team I once played against. The man's name was Evan Morris, but such was his tactical ruthlessness that he was known throughout the cricket pitches of Dyfed and into parts of Clwyd as Evan the Terrible. Of equal significance was the fact that his team's wicket-keeper, who was also the local undertaker, was known as Dai the Death. But the main perk of being the fielding captain is not in this exercise of petty megalomania. It is in leading your side on and off the field at the start and finish of each session.

Obviously it looks good to be the one at the head of these fine examples of virile athleticism, but the Compleat Captain is not, of course, interested in glory for its own sake. Being first on and first off has other benefits. If you field before tea, being first off gives you the chance to be first into the queue at the tea-urn, and, if you field after tea, being first back on again is the only known way to avoid having to buy raffle tickets and with it the chance to win a 20p box of liquorice allsorts for an outlay of only 40p. Two small victories to add to the list of successes of the season, which may or may not include a whole number in the wins column.

The good captain makes his tactics clear. How many times have we heard Brian Johnston or Trevor Bailey commenting microphonically that they cannot understand why the captain has done what he has just done. Or worse still, how he has let something happen. Captains do not let things happen, not even a victory. They imprint their personalities on a game and go positively to defeat. I happened to watch a match somewhere in the Midlands one overcast Saturday afternoon very early in May. The home side were captained by a young man with all the kit, who, I was told, was the newly-appointed club vice-captain who was having his first game as captain that very afternoon. Well, it became clear after a very short time that the poor boy would never make the grade as a leader. He lost the toss by calling wrongly, and yet was invited to bat. He put himself in as opener, despite the fact that he knew the opposition had a very quick opening bowler who could exploit the conditions superbly, and for an hour and a half he and the rest of his side struggled for runs. It was not until the fifth wicket fell, with the score on 53, that the sun emerged from behind the clouds and the big fast bowler (5 for 19) was put down at fine leg for a rest. The captain was still there, on 30, when his no. 7 came out to join him. There was just over half an hour till tea, and the leg-spinner came on at the heavy roller end. Twenty minutes later, the score was 102 for 5, with the no. 7, a cricketer after my own heart, not out 8 after two well-placed very late cuts between first and second slip. The captain, playing unnecessarily aggressively I felt, had reached 67 not out. The no. 7 now realised that tea was not much more than ten minutes away, and began playing quite sensibly for his average. The captain hammered on, apparently oblivious of the tactical niceties of the game. Three minutes later he was caught on the mid-wicket boundary for 72. At tea, the home side were 119 for 6, with no. 7 not out 9, a magnificent performance. The clouds were beginning to gather again, and clearly the right move would have been to bat on to earn the draw.

The captain declared. Quite obviously the power had gone to his head. I could see the local committee men shaking their heads in sorrow that matters should have come to this. The bowling was to be opened, as usual, by a burly left-hander who I was told was the local vet, who had opened the bowling there in every match for the past eleven years. Each season he had taken as many as 15 wickets for an average of well under 40 apiece, bowling down the hill for up to 20 overs at a time. Then quite suddenly, old men sat up in their chairs and the scorer broke his pencil in amazement. The vet was measuring out his run-up from the other end! What was the captain thinking of? Had Messrs Johnston or Bailey been there, kitted out as usual with earphones and a piece of chocolate cake sent in by a listener from Purley, they too would have expressed puzzlement at the captain's tactics. But worse was yet to come.

The vet took 2 for 9 in three overs, his best return for four years, and then he was taken off. The captain put on a rather weedy-looking individual, apparently a purveyor of off-breaks and top-spinners of uncertain pedigree, and positioned himself at mid-on. The first three balls were hit for four as the bowler struggled to find a length, a search with no more real hope of success than that of the conquistadores for El Dorado. The fourth ball, no better than the rest, was mis-hit by the batsman straight to the captain, who managed to hang on to the easy chance. The fifth ball went harmlessly through to the wicket-keeper, but the final ball must have pitched on the rough spot caused by years of the vet's follow-through. It reared up from a length and the batsman could only fend it off weakly but uppishly straight to mid-on again. Our worst suspicions were now confirmed, because the captain, in holding on to this most simple of catches, dislocated his thumb and had to retire from the game. The vet, as senior pro, took over as captain.

When the skipper returned from the hospital with his thumb strapped up, the opposition had moved from 36 for 4 to 108 for 5, with the vet, bowling from his favourite end, now boasting an analysis of 2 for 51 in twelve overs. Throughout the afternoon he had placed his field positively and changed the bowling at the other end with all the visible cunning and originality that one expects of a true leader, but in the end the opposition were proving just a little too strong. A few overs later, the winning hit was made, and the home side slid graciously to defeat. I must say that the responsibility for the defeat must lie with the injured captain, whose slow batting, early declaration and bizarre man-ipulation of the bowling clearly failed to establish a winning position. By the time that fate allowed the vet to step in and apply orthodox and positive captaincy to his side's efforts, it was too late to stem the tide.

I hope I have proved that leadership and victory are inextric-ably linked. Strong leadership leads to victories. Victories, whether big or small, personal or communal, lead to a thoroughly satisfying few hours in the 'Ploughman's Arms' at the end of the day. The only problem is that the captain does not always get the credit he really deserves, especially from the landlord, who deals only in cash. Defeat is an orphan, but victory has many claimants to the paternity. Such is the complexity of our summer game that those who often successfully claim responsibility for victory (but inevitably dissociate themselves entirely from the monotony of regular defeats) are men who do not even feature on the team sheets at the start of the game. These are the three wise monkeys of cricket, the umpire, the scorer and the groundsman.

6
UMPIRING, SCORING AND GROUNDSMANSHIP

It has already been noted in Chapter 5 that the value of any player to his side is not judged by cricketing ability alone. A player who fits in with the needs of the side will be selected, and the needs of the side vary from club to club and from village to village. Despite the fact that we have tended so far to concentrate on the development of playing skills or the camouflaging of minor technical shortcomings, there comes a time in every cricketer's career when the hard truth must be faced. Fitting in with the needs of the side may not be limited to active participation. It will also inevitably involve dealing in those black arts of the cricket field, Umpiring, Scoring and Groundsmanship.

These aspects of cricket must not be looked upon as chores to be avoided or even as necessary evils to be tolerated if evasive action has been unsuccessful. They are opportunities to be exploited. They represent chances to make a positive contribution to the match which may not be possible in any other way. They are ways of making your team need you. In salesman's language (and after all you are trying all the time to sell yourself both to your team-mates and to your opponents as a key member of the side), you have a chance to sell Features and Benefits. There must be Features of your Umpiring that bring Benefits to your team. There can very easily be Features of your Scoring that can give direct Benefit to your own performance on the field, and Features of Groundsmanship that can produce remarkable Benefits for the side batting first. Let us examine these three peripheral cricketing activities in greater detail.

'. . . those black arts of the cricket field . . .'

Umpiring

Whenever two impartial umpires are not available at the start of a match, it becomes necessary for one or more of the batting team to stand in judgement, one at the bowler's end and one at square leg, over the batting frailties of his team-mates. This can cause serious personal problems for the umpire unless he is truly impartial, i.e. unless he always favours the batting side. It must be remembered by any aspiring umpire that he is bound to be considered incompetent by some of the players at some stage in the game. In order to minimise his difficulties, he must therefore make sure that he is consistently biased against one side or the other, and the laws of survival dictate that the side he should be biased against is the opposition. Nothing is more likely to abbreviate a promising playing career than giving your own captain out 'handled the ball' for adjusting his abdominal protector. Nothing will improve your chances of a regular place more than refusing to acknowledge the existence of the lbw law while your opening pair are attempting to build a reply to 186 for 2 off 20 overs.

Chapter 2 failed, I regret to say, to give details of the correct garb for an umpire. However, what we are looking for now is not the correct garb for an umpire *per se* (white coat, black trousers, comfortable shoes, half a dozen pebbles) but the correct garb for a cricketer pressed into duty as an umpire, which is of course quite a different thing. A cricketer standing briefly as umpire needs to indicate, by his dress as well as his gestures, that he is not the real thing, that he is there under sufferance and that all decisions are final if not accurate. So he needs to wear his full cricket kit, minus pads, bat and gloves of course, and just a short-sleeved white sweater rather than an umpire's coat. This will make him virtually indistinguishable from any member of the fielding side, which will cause thoroughly satisfying confusion during his time stationed at square leg. If he also puts on (and then refuses to take off) all jerseys and caps discarded by perspiring bowlers, the confusion will be compounded to the inevitable benefit of the batsmen.

An umpire really has only four significant tasks to perform during the match. The first is to count the number of balls in each over, a computation which may be affected by his second responsibility, which is to send signals back to the scorer signifying the fairness and the quantity of what is going on. His third task is to stand in judgement over the batsmen and decide whether they will live or whether they will die, and his final job is the most important — to call a halt to the match in time for tea.

Counting the number of balls in each over ought not to be difficult. There are only six balls to count under normal circumstances, and even the feeblest mathematician in the team ought to be able to count up to six with reasonable accuracy. However, what makes this particular chore more complicated is the sheer monotony of it. After standing virtually motionless for half an hour or so, counting up to six balls tends to cause the same problems as counting up to six sheep, viz. you tend to fall asleep. Breaking the monotony by giving somebody out from time to time is an admirable idea in theory, but as in practice it will be your own batsmen you are sacrificing at the altar of your boredom, there may be repercussions back in the pavilion which may well involve looking for somewhere else to play cricket in future. A better way of adding a little interest to the task of counting up to six is to call 'Wide' and 'No-ball' now and again, which means you will have to count up to seven sometimes.

It is precisely because this counting procedure is so boring that all umpires use something to help them calculate the six-ball over accurately. Unless you are Anne Boleyn who, as any student of Tudor England will know, had six fingers on one hand, you will not have enough digits to count manually to six. Most umpires use pebbles, nuts and bolts, sticks or matches to help them remember how far through the over they are. One umpire of my acquaintance used miniature brandy bottles, which were full at the start of the innings but somewhat emptier at the end. The accuracy of his counting was never in doubt but his ability to favour the batting side with absolute consistency became seriously impaired by the time the fourth or fifth bottle was empty, so that the regular flow of wides, no-balls and not-outs tended to become infested with doubtful run-outs and one case of a batsman being given out lbw while he was attempting to take guard. The only thing that should never be used to count the balls is money. The clanking of coins as each ball is bowled confirms the ugly suspicion that the umpire has been bribed.

If counting up to six is the main mental activity of the umpire, the main physical activity is in giving signals to the scorer, signals which indicate who is doing what and to whom. It is obviously essential that all signals are clearly understood by the scorers if confusion is to be avoided and a fair result is to be achieved. It is also obviously essential, therefore, that as soon as his team appears to be on the way to yet another silver medal the umpire makes his signals as Delphic as possible, so that reinterpretation at the end of the innings can, if necessary, make sure that a fair result is not achieved. When your team appears to be all out for 34, constructive, retrospective umpiring can make a vital difference to your prospects of victory. A not untypical conversation between umpire and opposition scorer can go like this.

UMPIRE (strolling into pavilion, bails in pocket) 'Bit early for tea, isn't it? Why have we come in now?'
OPPOSITION SCORER (a puny sixteen-year-old bespectacled know-

all) 'Your team is all out for 34. Wilmot (J.P.), left arm over the wicket 7 for 19, top scorer extras with 11.'

UMPIRE 'All out. That's ridiculous. What about Bill?'

OPPOSITION SCORER 'If you are referring to W. Renshaw, who batted number seven wearing, as I recall, a Quidnuncs cap and two left leg guards, he was c. Rogers (C.T.) b. Wilmot 1.'

UMPIRE 'Rubbish. I was umpiring and I should know. How could he be caught off his thigh? He retired hurt after being hit very hard off a no-ball from your Mr Wilmot. I distinctly remember calling no-ball, and our scorer acknowledged my call. Didn't you, Jack?'

JACK (who is used to all this and is even now revising his scorebook with rubber and pencil) 'Oh yes.'

UMPIRE 'There you are then. That makes us 35 for 9, extras top scorer with 12 and Wilmot 6 for 19. Is Bill fit to resume his innings?'

OPPOSITION SCORER 'But why did you put your finger up when our lads appealed?'

UMPIRE 'Did I? That must have been the moment when I spotted that Red Admiral fluttering across the pitch, and I put my finger up for it to rest on. And to think you thought I was giving Bill out!' (He glances at the scorebook.) 'What about that six that Fred hit? Why isn't that in the book?'

OPPOSITION SCORER 'What six? F.D.J. Smith, if he is the player you are talking about, was b. Wilmot for 4. That four was a lucky snick through the slips.'

UMPIRE 'That was a six, not a four.'

OPPOSITION SCORER 'Then why did you signal a four? I distinctly saw you waving your arm from side to side in the approved manner for indicating a boundary four.'

UMPIRE 'Nonono. I'm afraid you have once again missed the point. I was waving my arm from side to side to get rid of the Red Admiral, which had by then outstayed its welcome. After that I signalled a six. 37 for 9.'

And so on. It is usually at this point that the opposition scorer crumbles into unmanly tears, and a complete rewrite is on the cards. By the time tea is over, the score will be about 65 for 8, and we will bat on. Only the umpires will be changed, to protect the innocent.

Despite the best intentions of even the most flagrantly unfair umpire, there will be moments when into each life a wicket must fall. Even your own players will be out and there will be nothing you can do about it. However, at these moments of crisis for the umpire, to say nothing of the batsman who misses a straight one, you will be greatly reassured if you are confident about the Laws of Cricket. It will not have escaped the notice of the more astute reader that we have reached Chapter 6 already without more than a passing mention of the laws of the game. This is a deliberate strategy, as anybody who wants to learn them has only to write to the MCC enclosing postal order and s.a.e. to receive his own copy of the Laws of Cricket by return of post. What they tell you is what is right and what is wrong. They don't tell you what actually happens in a game of cricket, and a man who goes out to umpire with only the rule book to guide him is as likely to succeed as a man who understands the principle of the jet engine and on the strength of that knowledge tries to land a Jumbo at Heathrow. The Laws of Cricket are what the astute umpire turns to when all else has failed, and there are only two areas that need concern him.

The first point to study is the repeated mention of the phrase 'In the opinion of the umpire'. The Laws of Cricket basically state that if, in the opinion of the umpire, black is white, then black is white no matter how often the captains, players, scorers, masseurs and tea lady may try to put the contrary point of view. Umpiring is Power. Umpire Rules O.K.

The other problem area is the lbw law. Since the 1980 Revised Version of the Laws, the lbw law (now Law 36, going up the charts after many years as Law 39) states in essence that in almost every circumstance the batsman is not out. The official view is that anybody good enough not to be bowled by a straight one should not be penalised merely because the position of his legs was not as recommended in the coaching manuals. There are only three circumstances in which to give the batsman out.

'OW BE WHAT ?

'... in almost every circumstance the batsman is not out...'

1)   If it's the last over before tea, and you are hungry.

2)   If the batsman in question will go above you in the club averages unless you do something about it pretty quickly.

3)   If the bowler has already threatened to tear you limb from limb and feed the pieces to his ferrets next time you turn down a lbw appeal.

The final duty of the umpire is to get the innings into a satisfactory state by teatime so that the match remains finely balanced, and more importantly so that the fielding side does not succumb to the temptation to 'play on till we get them all out' rather than take tea for which umpires and batsmen are longing at the predestined hour. This is a heavy responsibility and to carry it out successfully the umpire must wear a watch. Too often, unfortunately, an umpire finds himself wearing four or five watches as batsmen and fielders realise halfway through the proceedings that they have forgotten to leave theirs in the pavilion, and as no two watches ever agree precisely the umpire's job of timing the tea interval is made unnecessarily complicated.

Once the umpire has decided a) what time tea is to be and b) which watch he will go by, he must then decide what a suitable teatime score would be. All then proceeds serenely until about ten minutes before tea (umpires without watches can usually tell when zero hour is approaching by the smell of cucumber, rock buns and tea bags drifting like a cloud of tear gas across the pitch). At this point the umpire realises he has three or four overs in which to take four wickets or score 50 runs or both. Provided the umpire's tactics roughly coincide with those of the batting side (of which he is, let us remind ourselves, a member), the required total is usually reached, and nos. 9, 10 and 11 either score yet another duck or else take quick singles off a succession of wides and no-balls, and somehow never quite get run out. At times like these, the reluctant umpire can truly feel that all is for the best in this best of all possible worlds.

Scoring

If you have no intention of ever being made to umpire, confident in the knowledge that your Nagging Injury (blindness in both eyes) disqualifies you from the rigours of adjudication, you may still find the hours that your side spends batting filled with something other than lying in the sunshine gazing at the village policeman's nineteen-year-old daughter. You may be excused umpire duties indefinitely, but this only makes Scoring even more difficult to avoid. It is however much more personally satisfying, even if it lacks the opportunities afforded by Umpiring to satisfy your megalomaniac cravings.

The job of the Scorer is to record accurately what is happening statistically on the pitch. This requires mathematical abilities beyond Ph.D. standard, 'O' level semaphore (to identify the intentions of your colleague who is umpiring) and stoic calm not to feel outraged by the blindingly unfair fact that a snick through

TWO POINT SEVEN
NOUGHT EIGHT
RECURRING—

WISDEN 1957   120

MALTDRAIN'S Mediocre ALE

'... *mathematical abilities beyond Ph.D. standard* ...'

the slips can frequently mean more runs in the scorebook than a majestic cover drive. Cricket is a great leveller and the scorebook is the proof of the level to which we all too often sink.

It is very rare indeed that a yoga-practising Senior Wrangler from the Royal Signals Corps is available to score for you, so the average Sunday XI makes do with what it has, i.e. a no. 10 or 11 hoping he won't get roped in for the job. The only proven way to get out of it once you have been commissioned is to break every pencil in sight, and then nobody does the scoring. But that is a very shortsighted attitude. Better by far to volunteer for the job and to put it to practical use. Consider the perks: a) you sit on a chair; b) the chair will be somewhere warm; and c) you have access to all the scores in every match your team has played this season. What more can a man ask?

At the heart of the scoring system is the fact that scorers work in pairs, just like umpires. The two scorebooks are supposed to tally, and if they do that is the proof that the score is correct. The total number of runs scored off the bowlers plus the total number of extras equals the total scored by the batting side, or at least it is meant to. In practice it rarely does, even with a skilled practitioner handling the HB. This gives you an opportunity to inflate the total or at least destroy their opening bowler's analysis. Extras is always the repository of an extra run or two. It depends upon which of their players has annoyed you most, one of their bowlers or perhaps the wicket-keeper, as to how the required runs are stacked in the scorebook. I tend to favour the gambit of giving wides and no-balls to any bowler who looks too good in the scorebook, but the option of loading the byes column is open to any scorer who considers the wicket-keeper too flashy by half.

A good scorer can be worth at least half a dozen runs to his side, which is probably five more than his worth to them as a player. But, then again, the real El Dorado of Scoring is the free and unlimited access to the scorebook that it affords. Many is the player I have known who went into a match with a season's average of 2.08 and finished the day with an average of 17.34, despite scoring only 3 when his turn came to bat. The secret lies in the fact that all cricket scores are entered into the scorebook in pencil, and all scorers are issued with a rubber to correct mistakes. And was not last Sunday's duck against High Dudgeon a mistake? You should never have played that flashing cover drive against the leg-spinner, especially as it pitched on leg stump and had hit the top of middle stump before your bat had completed its downswing in some other part of the pitch. 'Never make the same mistake twice' is a rule my old uncle impressed upon me from the time when I was but a babe in arms. The joy of scoring is that you need never even make the same mistake once, as one sweep of the rubber can eradicate retrospectively all errors made with one sweep of the bat throughout the season.

My particular recommendation is that attention is paid to your fielding. When the High Dudgeon XI are in the field, it is commonplace for there to be nobody at the scorebook who knows the name of all the players in the side. The plaintive cry of 'Bowler's name!' from the scorebox end is a familiar one to all village cricketers, although I must confess I have not recently heard it ringing out across Lord's or the Oval. It follows of course that if the scorers have to be advised of the bowler's name, then there is virtually no chance that they will know the name of the fielder, in the unlikely event that any catches offered actually stick. That is why scorers do not usually put down the fielder's name in the scorebook, just the word 'caught'. A quick glance at the back pages of any village scorebook will confirm this point, and any scorer worth his salt will take the opportunity of filling in the blanks with his own name, until he builds for himself a useful, but not over-ostentatious, tally of catches, and with it the reputation as a fielder as snappy as a crocodile sandwich.

The Holy Grail of the cricketer, from Viv Richards and Dennis Lillee down to you and me, is being Top Of The Averages. Many is the cricketer of whom it has been said, 'He never played for his average', but these are always the people who averaged 86.97 with the bat and 9.24 with the ball, for whom topping the averages year in and year out comes as easily as getting into the same pair of flannels year in and year out. The rest of us are judged on our averages and the biggest thrill available to the run of the mill Sunday cricketer (at least on days when the village policeman's daughter is not making the teas) is to score more runs, take more wickets or catch more catches than ever before, and thereby Improve the Average. Unfortunately, the very definition of the word 'average', and its methods of calculation, means that you will in the normal run of things turn in below average performances as often as you will improve the situation.

Unless, of course, you are the Scorer.

Groundsmanship

It has been suggested, by people whose lack of mathematical and cricketing skills denies them the chance of ever hitting the top, that the averages are unfair and that there are more constructive ways of looking at a player's value to the side. Raffle tickets sold per run scored is a useful criterion, which will show up the true pillars of the side (50 raffle tickets sold, 2 runs scored: average 25.00) against the flashy self-seekers (2 raffle tickets sold, three more books eaten by dog, 78 scored out of a total of 93 which gave the team victory by 2 runs: average 0.026). Another is runs scored multiplied by time wasted between tea and the start of the last twenty overs, which is a crucial period for a fielding side trying desperately to hold out at least till the pubs open. A couple of bootlaces undone, a fly in the eye and encouraging young children to play behind the bowler's arm can be worth quite a few minutes and therefore many more runs to your side. However, if we are looking for the truest way to judge a man's value to his team we must first of all ask the basic question: 'Is he the groundsman?'

If the answer is yes, then he is of value to the side. Groundsmanship is difficult, boring and physically tiring and anybody who can be persuaded to undertake such duties in order to allow 21 other people to trample all over his good work deserves not only a permanent place in the side but also a free rock-bun at teatime and first crack at the scorebook every time he plays. Groundsmanship is a specialised form of gardening, and those of us who play cricket largely to get out of mowing our own lawns find it a cruel irony of fate that there is an awful lot more lawn to be mowed before the game gets under way.

The duties of the groundsman are fairly straightforward, it is the achievement of these duties that is more complicated. All he has to do is to prepare the ground so that a game can be played on it at least once a week. This involves preparing the square, choosing the wicket to be used, applying mower, roller and water in the correct proportions, marking the pitch, painting the sightscreen, preparing the outfield and forecasting the weather and the strength of the opposition with equal accuracy. If he does all this correctly, the game is as good as won before you start.

Preparing the square is the least of a groundsman's worries. Most groundsmen are taking over their duties from somebody who has at last found not only a cast-iron excuse for backing down but also a successor, so most new groundsmen have a square already in position, crying out for a quick roll, mow and water. If any budding groundsman is reading this chapter hoping for advice on how to carve a cricket pitch out of waste land or the side of a coal tip, then you've picked up the wrong book. Landscape gardening is not part of my brief. On the other hand, those groundsmen who already have a cricket pitch, square and all, to look after, can read on in the certain knowledge that new light will be cast upon their problems.

Your first job as groundsman is to get to know the pitch. Learn how much slope there is from left to right and north to south. Look for the uneven patches on the square, and if there are no uneven patches make one yourself. Watch how the ground drains, and notice where and when the sun sets at the different times of the summer. This information is vital in selecting the right wicket for each match and for selecting the right team for the right wicket. Late in August, when the sun sets earlier and behind the bowler's arm at the bottom end of the ground, it is often advisable to select the wicket that will bring the sun most directly into the game. Consider whether or not your main strike bowler that day will be the left-arm over or right-arm over, and decide which of two adjoining wickets will be the most suitable. On overcast weekends, a wicket at the bottom of the slope (all squares are on a slope: this is because the Earth is round) will be wetter and of more value to the off-spinner. When your star left-hander is playing, use a wicket that will reduce the distance from wicket to boundary for his well-known cover drive, and make sure there's a nasty dip in the outfield just there that will make the fielder racing round to cut off said cover drive stumble and miss it.

Large trees are another feature of most grounds that can be put to good use. For many years I have played a match against a village team in Sussex whose beautiful ground is dominated by a large oak tree on the third man boundary. The village's star batsman has one particularly strong shot, which is a cut to third man, so even our wandering eleven, not known for tactical astuteness, knew to put a man at third man when the second wicket fell. Two years ago, we played a rain-affected match against them, and, as evening drew on, they needed 20 to win as the last pair came together. Their no. 11, who clearly was unlikely ever to reach the shortlist for an England tour to Australia, walked slowly out to join that star batsman Stan Something, 42 not out. At this point, the thunder rolled and a bolt of lightning cracked straight into the oak tree, which was at wide mid-on while the bowling was at the far end. Despite this elemental intervention, the last man survived the one remaining ball of the over. We now had the problem of taking the last wicket before the rain came down, with Stan facing.

Our opening bowler walked back to his mark and looked about him. Just as he started his run up he noticed there was no third man. He stopped.

'Hey captain,' he enquired with all the gentility normally associated with fast bowlers. 'Where's third man gone to?'

'Fine leg,' came the answer.

'Well, tell him to move back to third man. I don't need a fine leg for this chap.'

Fine leg joins the conversation at this point.

'I'm not standing under a tree that's just been struck by lightning. I've got metal studs on my boots.'

'Look here, sunshine,' said the bowler affably. 'I doubt whether even 20,000 volts could make you move quick enough to be much use to me anywhere in the field, but the only place you might be of any value at all is under that tree, so go there.'

'No.'

More thunder rumbles across the sky.

'OK. I'll put somebody else there. Captain, can I move Bob down to third man and put Jack . . . .'

'No. Bob won't go there either.'

A flash of lightning split the sky just to the north of the ground.

'Nor will anybody else. Even their no. 11 batsman has taken off his helmet because it is made of metal. He'd rather be killed by you than by Mother Nature. He says his insurance cover is better.'

So we played on without a third man. Stan hit the first five balls of the over for four and the match was won minutes before the heavens opened and flooded the pitch.

'Useful tree that,' said their captain in the pub afterwards. 'Since our groundsman suggested we put the lightning conductor in it, our pavilion has never been struck and Stan has won quite a few games for us.'

Mowing the pitch is another vital factor of groundsmanship. It is always essential that the outfield looks good before a game. The opposition are impressed if they see neat wide bands reminiscent of Wembley or Trent Bridge criss-crossing the outfield, and they may just be worried that this professional approach to groundsmanship as expressed in the mowing will carry over to the performance of the local side as well. Seeds of doubt are as valuable as seeds of grass in the psychological warfare of cricket. One useful tip regarding mowing the outfield is to do it on the morning of the match, and not to rake the cuttings behind the boundary until after the captains have tossed. If your team is batting, immediately rake all the grass beyond the boundary line. If the opposition have elected to bat, leave the piles of grass cuttings inside the boundary. They ought to stop a four or two before tea is taken, at which time you rake back the grass, a job you were unable to complete earlier because you were otherwise occupied fielding. It's all so simple when you know how.

The weather forecast plays a very important part in groundsmanship, because the choice of wicket will obviously be affected by whether or not rain, sun, smog or earthquake is expected. On a muggy day, when the swing bowlers will be moving it about a bit, you will want to ensure that the inevitable snicks through the slips don't go for four. Choose the wicket with the longest boundary in that direction. During a long dry spell, nurture an unwatered patch just on a length for your back-of-the-hand spinner, and don't sweep away the dust. Use of the very heavy roller during a particularly wet month can delay the start of the match while you all risk herniation by trying to pull the roller out of the mud, and the resulting indentation should be just far enough up the wicket to give your opening bowler's bumpers a roller coaster effect as they shoot up out of the dip straight into opposition eyebrows.

Marking out the pitch is a final duty of the groundsman. I once turned up at a ground where the stumps had been put in on pitch 3 at one end and on pitch 4 at the other. This meant that bowling straight would have been no good at all. Even our somewhat wayward bowlers would have noticed the discrepancy after an over or two, but as we were asked to bat first the mistake was realised by the home team even before the match got under way. We lost, but never let it be said that an astute cricketer learns nothing from defeat. Pitch your stumps so much out of line that everybody immediately notices and all that will happen is that the opposition will laugh at your team's incompetence, double in confidence and as soon as the wicket is marked out correctly they will slaughter you. Pitch your stumps just a couple of inches or so out of line, and nobody will notice over 22 yards, except the opposition bowler (taking a day off from playing for Warwickshire II) who will not be able to understand why he is straying persistently down the leg side and being hit for four by semi-competent geriatrics, when yesterday he took 4 for 26 at Edgbaston. Subtle groundsmanship could set a promising career back by years, which in this case is fine unless you happen to be a supporter of Warwickshire II.

Umpiring, Scoring and Groundsmanship are all active participatory aspects of cricket. Without umpires, scorers and groundsmen, the match could not take place, and even with them one sometimes wishes the match was not taking place. However, if disillusionment or terminal incompetence has set in so totally that any influence on the outcome of the match is no longer looked for, there is only one way to satisfy the cravings for the drug that is cricket. That is by spectating.

7
THE COMPLEAT SPECTATOR

People who watch cricket do so because it is the only way to satisfy their emotional involvement with the game and/or the participants. There are many different ways of spectating, and the joy of this particular pastime is that it can be done at all levels of the game by even the most incompetent. I myself have had the honour of spectating at Test Match level on several occasions, and I think I acquitted myself with credit. It is therefore with no lack of experience or confidence that I pen these few words on the Art Of Spectating.

Spectating at the highest level of the game is a privilege afforded to only a few, say 150,000 during the normal run of five Tests in a summer, not to mention the millions who watch via the electronic mysteries of television and Richie Benaud, so I feel it would be out of place to devote too many column inches to such a recondite activity in a work of such broad general interest as this. However, if only to point out the differences between spectating at first-class matches and doing likewise at the annual tussle between High Dudgeon and Lower Scoring, a few words on the professional game are called for.

First-class spectating is a professional game because you have to pay to participate. Unless you have managed to achieve the exalted position of Member of your County Club, you will have to pay at the gate every time you wish to add to your career aggregate of matches watched. Once inside the ground, further opportunities for spending money leap at you from all sides — scorecards, cushions, ice-creams, cricket tea-towels, rosettes etc. — so all but the most skilled may discover that spectating is a hobby which, like polo and getting divorced in California, should be confined to the super-rich. There are, however, ways of earning money as a spectator which can go some way towards covering the cost of a David Gower poster or an Old Trafford pork pie.

Probably the most lucrative way of watching cricket, if you are prepared to tolerate the social stigma that goes with it, is to be a commentator. Commentators get free tickets to the match, the chance to tell everybody about what they have just seen and a better tea than the players. It is fortunate for this breed of men that they go about their tasks only at first-class matches. Anybody who enjoyed such privileges and never stopped talking into the bargain would have a limited life expectancy at a village game. This may be the reason why commentators are such a misunderstood body of men, and why they feature so regularly in many of the ribald songs performed by the crowds at the matches where they commentate. They do, however, make the professional spectator's life far easier in that without the presence of the electronic media at the match being spectated, many of the more interesting and fashionable activities of a spectator's day cannot take place.

For example, why bother to wave a banner reading 'Hallo Mum', if the Mum referred to therein is not able to see it wave on television? No commentators, no television: no television, no banner-waving. It all follows with inexorable logic. Commentators are also therefore directly responsible for such crowd behaviour as Waving To The TV Camera, Streaking, Beating Up The Umpires In The Pavilion at Centenary Tests, and of course, Playing Transistor Radios Too Loud At The Vauxhall End. Nevertheless, commentators can be seen as serving a social purpose. In the ultimate selection for eternity's Good Chaps v. The Rest, commentators might be the last to be chosen, but chosen they are. We may be able to hold them responsible for the rapid decline in the literate use of English, as demonstrated in a banner reading 'England Are Great' or 'Botham Bites Yer Bails', but they also promote sales of television and radio sets, MCC ties, prep school joke books and Teach Yourself Australian cassette programmes. An innumerable multitude of electronics assembly workers, haberdashers, publishers and colonial professors are kept in business purely by the efforts of Britain's cricket commentators, and this is a wonderful achievement for which they should receive fulsome praise.

One of the most noticeable features of a Test Match these days is the soundtrack. Cricket used to operate as almost a silent movie, with well-groomed, well-hatted spectators staring mutely at the match that was unfolding before them, with only the occasional massed 'Oooh!' or respectful applause punctuating the funereal quality of the afternoon. It was as though the clothing worn by the cricketers was so frivolously white that the crowd had to present a collective dour blackness to restore the equilibrium of the afternoon. The change seems to have dated from the 1960s, that swinging decade which changed the face of both the Universe and cricket. The inventions of T-shirts and canned beer were the pivotal events, along with the discovery that cricket cannot survive on gate money alone. This meant that if cricket did not need the crowds, the crowds also did not need cricket, so when they came to watch, they came on their own terms. They began to enjoy themselves as much as to enjoy the cricket.

The introduction in the 1970s and 1980s of helmets, multi-coloured logos on bats and gloves, and all the other paraphernalia of modern cricket (see Chapter 2) has accelerated the trend, and crowds now display individuality within the team framework of the sport of spectating that could not have been guessed at even 30 years ago. One has only to study the brilliant way the movement behind the bowler's arm is given individual touches by each person who catches the batsman's eyes; how a new spectator who has not yet been subjected to the communal disapproval of players and umpires will settle exactly behind the bowler's arm and move only when that bowler is running in to bowl; and how the ground authorities persist in building stands behind the bowler's arm so that even Madame Tussaud's waxworks could disrupt play if the sun comes out or the clouds roll by. The environment for constructive spectating has never been better than it is today, and manipulation of the soundtrack, vocal and otherwise, to the cricket on the pitch is the way to make it more constructive than ever.

For the past few seasons, leading spectators have armed themselves with large numbers of beer cans and referees' whistles, while a few musical souls have emerged as leading exponents of the Klaxon horn, than which there are few lovelier sounds at a cricket match. Together these rhythmical people have created an orchestrated background to the cricket, a background which often penetrates so insidiously into the consciousness of other less musically gifted spectators that it sometimes seems that the cricket is the background to the music. Perhaps this is the

'... a balletic art...'

direction of the future. Cricket will become a balletic art like synchronised swimming or ice dancing, and the music will decide the tempo and the choreography of the game. This development cannot be completed, however, until the crowds begin to play recognisable tunes, and thus take the major step from gifted amateurs to grafting professionals. All the spectators have to do is to play a tune that is in copyright, and the BBC will be liable to pay author's royalties on the tunes they inadvertently but inevitably broadcast. The Massed Beer Cans and Refs' Whistle Symphony Orchestra in the free seats at long-on has therefore to work out a deal in advance with the songwriters whose Greatest Hits they intend to hammer their way through, and then they must play lustily for five days to earn at least enough to cover the cost of the beer cans and the contents thereof. This is clearly going to become another effective way of earning money as a cricket spectator. Furthermore, it is not only legal but it also fulfils the moral responsibility that the broadcasters and the lovers of cricket have for the financial well-being of those whose constructive musical imaginations have created the sounds that have replaced leather on willow as the traditional noises of cricket.

*   *   *

Enough of the professional spectator, whose skills and ambitions are far divorced from those of the people who gather around the boundary boards of the High Dudgeon pitch on Saturday and Sunday afternoons. These people are the real lovers of cricket, for they willingly sacrifice an afternoon when they could be gardening, painting and decorating or oiling children's bicycles just to watch a game of cricket. From the cricketer's point of view too, playing in front of tens of thousands at Lord's on a Saturday afternoon is quite different from playing in front of sometimes as many as ten on a village green. For a start it is rare to hear refs' whistles and klaxon horns subtly pounding across the greensward at High Dudgeon, although I do remember one bowler colliding with the umpire in his delivery stride, causing both to retire hurt, when a four-year-old accidentally activated the burglar alarm on a

BMW parked at square leg. Secondly, it is rare to be asked for your autograph by a swarm of young boys as you leave the pitch at teatime. Thirdly, it is unlikely that a pitch invasion as the winning hit is made will force cricketers and umpires alike to sprint for the safety of the pavilion. Fourthly, it is probable that the pavilion will be structurally incapable of providing safety if ever that unlikely pitch invasion takes place.

Finally, there is the biggest single difference between the professional and the amateur spectator. Most professionals are male. Most amateurs are female. The problem has been that when two cricket matches are available to be spectated, the professional will invariably choose the 'better' of the two games, i.e. the first-class one. Therefore, the only people left to spectate at the other type of cricket match are the amateurs, and the only amateurs who volunteer to watch what some ignoramuses have even categorised as boring, i.e. cricket, are those who have some personal interest in one or more of the participants. The participants being almost exclusively male and cricket not being an activity at the forefront of the sexual revolution, it follows that those who have some personal interest in said participants are almost exclusively female.

This is wonderful news for those who get parked down at fine leg on a hot afternoon. Out there it is inevitable that a fielder will pay more attention to what is happening near at hand beyond the boundary boards rather than far away where batsman and bowler are locked in combat. Such a fielder will have an opportunity to revel in breathtaking views of anatomical delights visible only in outline through t-shirt and bikini top, while his colleagues crouch at second slip or short leg with only the smell of their nearest team-mate's socks to distract them from the game at hand. At times like these, cricket becomes unique among sports in that it is the only one with more players looking at the spectators than vice versa. If the spectator whose shape is distracting the players from the agenda for the afternoon does not belong to you, then this spectator affords nothing but enjoyment — a welcome addition to the pleasures of the day. If on the other hand, the spectator in question is your wife/girlfriend/daughter/grandmother, then action must be taken to ensure that such flagrant displays of uncovered flesh do not happen again. The spectators must be trained.

Cricketers need equipment (see Chapter 2), and so do spectators. So, ladies, read on. It is no good just turning up at a match and assuming everything will be provided. If you wish to watch the match, you need to be in full possession of your kit. On a typical afternoon, the spectator will need the following.

1) Rug. As a general rule of thumb, spectators sit down to do their spectating. Although there will probably be seats near the pavilion, it is an unchallengeable law of the Universe that these seats are filled by cricketers or their henchmen, the scorers. The only empty seats ever provided by the management are those which are unsafe for use. Many is the innocent visiting spectatorette who has parked her pert little bottom provocatively into an empty deck-chair only to have it collapse beneath her within seconds. This is because all cricket clubs set out all their fatally wounded seats in the most desirable spot in the shade of the lime-tree, in the hope that some naive visitor will administer the *coup de grâce* and have to pay for a new one. To avoid this extra expense, bring a rug to sit on.

2) Dogs and children. These are not compulsory, so people who do not already own either or both do not need to feel entirely excluded from the experiences of the afternoon. However, people who are already infested with these two species of pet always seem to bring them along to the game and often provide spares for the use of those who do not have their own.

3) Food. Remember that tea in the pavilion is scoffed by the participants, not the hangers-on. Also remember that if you bring the food, you will also need dog and excess child repellent (see 2 above).

4) Clothing. At least three complete sets of clothing are normally needed. The changeable climate means that anorak and wellies must be part of any clothes list for spectators, along with sunhat, sunglasses, jerseys, thermal underwear, Ambre Solaire, aspirin etc. A complete duplicate set of everything should also be packed in anticipation of the moment when a dog or infant

deposits something disgusting all over you. It is distressing to note how often spectators do not come kitted out for the match: some, especially those of the female variety in the 15 to 20 age bracket, turn up wearing little but see-through t-shirts and tightly-stretched shorts.

Once you have the kit all worked out, do not imagine that you are now completely ready to watch all the manifold and varied tragedies of village cricket. Spectating requires practice, and in this respect it is quite different from playing the game. As we have already seen (Chapter 3 — you should know your way about these pages well enough by now without me having to point you in the right direction all the time), time spent practising playing cricket is time wasted. Why bowl your best ball of the season in the nets? Why dismiss one of your own players with it, when it is much more fun to dispose of your teammates with a succession of ill-judged quick singles in a real game? Why play your only recognisable cover drive of the year in an indoor net in February? Spectating, on the other hand, is often improved by practice. There is nothing worse for a cricketer who has played his highest innings for four years (3 not out) to find that his personal spectator has slept through the whole thing, or was at the time rescuing an offspring from the stinging nettles. You must learn to concentrate.

If your cricketer is the type of player who likes to graft for his runs, for whom excitement is hitting the ball towards extra cover and calling 'wait', then you need to practise for one of his innings by watching something equally fast-moving. Maybe the traffic lights at the pedestrian crossing by the primary school would fit the bill. Or if that is too hectic try the BBC2 test card at 3.15 am. If he is of the brawny, vigorous variety, settle down to a clip from *The World About Us* showing hippopotami mating. Find something worth studying that will prepare you for the undiluted pleasures of watching your cricketer in action. And if you suffer from hay fever, take along the eye-drops. One blink and you may miss all the relevant action for the day, and unless you can truthfully say 'Yes I saw you', you will have to suffer hours of listening to your cricketer talking you through it, time after time after time. To practise for that, watch *Match Of The Day* every Saturday night for three seasons.

If you have the kit and are in peak spectating condition, you are now ready to test your skills in the crucible of reality. You are ready to be tried out as a spectator. At this juncture, a word of warning is called for. Cricket is a summer game, and the summer in England has occasionally brought with it the sunshine. Sunshine, meadows, rugs and a reasonable tea can often combine to cause drowsiness in even the most dedicated of spectators. This is fatal to successful spectating. Alertness is essential. It is no good lying asleep in the sun or slinking off to the pub for a quick one. You must not let your concentration waver for a second. Even one second, during which time Allan Wells or Carl Lewis could only move ten metres or so, is long enough for a three-year-old to waddle across to Daddy at second slip or for the assorted dogs inevitably present to indulge their sexual fantasies at third man. A mistake of such magnitude is enough for any woman to be banned forever by her cricketer from watching him play, and what a misfortune that would be.

Only once do I recall such an event being forgiveable. It was in the match between High Dudgeon and The Dirty Old Men, a wandering team of minimal ability. The Dirty Old Men were batting, and the sun was beating down from an azure sky. In those days the High Dudgeon no. 10 was a rich, good-looking chap called Charlie Hopkins, who at the age of 34 had neatly sidestepped the outstretched arms of many a young lady who had attempted to lure him into matrimony. In place of a wife, Charlie had hit on the brilliant alternative of a large Dalmatian dog which for some reason he had named after the captain of the 1953 Australians, Hassett. 'Dapper' is the adjective that springs to mind when Lindsay Hassett's name is mentioned, but dapper is not the word to describe his canine namesake. When this particular incident occurred, tea had already been taken and Hassett, having finished the fruit cake on behalf of the cricketers (in truth he had also started it) was looking for new fields to conquer. High Dudgeon were in the field and Charlie had entrusted Hassett to the care of one Christine, who had certain unmistakeable attributes which were no doubt appreciated by those who came into close contact with her, but who felt that there was only one activity less interesting than looking after dogs and that was watching cricket. Christine therefore fell asleep.

Hassett on the other hand was full of life. Pausing only momentarily to sniff indelicately up the dress of the village constable's nineteen-year-old daughter (see Chapter 6) Hassett bounded onto the pitch and indecently assaulted deep extra cover. Unaware of the damage this caused to his field placings, the captain of High Dudgeon carried on bowling. The ball was a slow long hop and the batsman played no stroke as it gently bumped against his pad. Simultaneously, deep extra cover and Charlie Hopkins attempted to rectify the situation vis-à-vis animal sex and shouted, 'Hassett!' Their captain, who had bent down to pick up the ball as it trickled back to him, was astonished to look up and see the umpire's finger rising inexorably skywards. For the first time in his career, he had won an lbw decision without even appealing. The batsman wandered forlornly pavilionwards with the look of a man who knows that the fates have conspired successfully against him. Hassett chose this moment to break off his tempestuous affair with deep extra, who obviously did not sufficiently resemble a Dalmatian bitch on heat. He took a friendly bite out of the defeated batsman's thigh pad as he cantered past, on his way to Christine's rug, where he fell suddenly and lengthily asleep. Thereafter the rot set in and a game that seemed won at 52 for 0 was lost. High Dudgeon won by 20 runs with three overs to spare. Hassett was made Man of the Match, and within two weeks the banns were up announcing the forthcoming marriage of Charles and Christine, an event which took place on the first Saturday after the end of the cricket season. Christine, who slept through the entire drama that had clinched her position as a Hopkins for several seasons to come, never did learn to become a great spectator, and her teas quickly became legendary for their toxicity. However, Charlie always had a smile on his face, so there must have been something about her that made her suitable material for a Compleat Cricketer's wife.

'... *took place on the first Saturday after the end of the cricket season...*'

The innate ability to make a tea so noxious that nobody asks you twice is another common, if anti-social, attribute of the Compleat Spectator. This Christine had, although I often wondered how she was able to keep her husband and the rapidly ensuing offspring so well-fed without somehow being able to turn on the same magic when it came to cricket teas. Why was her steak au poivre, which once I was privileged to taste at a private dinner party, so close to perfection, yet her ham sandwiches so curled at the edges? How could she be praised in four counties for the quality of her vichysoisse, and yet still stew the tea every Sunday afternoon? I put it down to the fact that she suffered from the culinary equivalent of big match nerves — great in the nets, but no good out in the middle.

In the quest to become the perfect spectator, there are yet more hurdles to overcome. The kit, the long hours of practice, the alertness and concentration are all necessary, but the final ingredient in the great spectator is the crucial one. It is sympathy. The *sine qua non* of a good spectator is to be sympathetic to your particular hero's problems. Try to look as though you really believe he will make fifty as he strides out to bat, and try to wipe off that sardonic grin as he explains on his return a few moments later how the fly got into his eye and made him miss a straight one. Show that you agree that the third ball of his second over would have hit leg stump if the batsman had not flukily edged it over long-on and into the river. Never let on that you spotted the googly even if he didn't. Above all, never imply on Monday morning that his stiffness is due to age and incompetence rather than the unexpected rigours of having to bat for as many as eleven balls the day before.

Sympathy is not confined to thoughtful looks and loving caresses. Whoever wrote 'Sticks and stones may break my bones, but words will never hurt me' was clearly not a cricketer. Statements like 'Your sweater's shrunk since last year' can hurt a man deeply. A man whose team has lost by ten wickets before tea should not have the knife turned in the wound by his personal spectator saying, 'Never mind, that means you will have time to paint the garage before nightfall.' Phrases like 'Daddy, I thought you were meant to stop the ball hitting those three sticks' or 'Little Jimmy did wee wee in your cricket boots' are also to be discouraged among the younger generation. Above all, never bring mothers or grandmothers to watch you play. They ran out of sympathy when you were six. They also have a fatal tendency to reveal unflattering secrets of your past at a time when they need to take what American psychiatrists would call 'a supportive stance'.

I remember the case of Geoff Barrow, a large amiable hulk of a man, who one day brought his mother to watch him play. Geoff opened the batting as usual, and after a couple of overs we were thinking in terms of him improving his batting average which even then stood at the unheard-of heights of 19.28. He was looking confident. That, need I say, was when disaster struck. The pitch was rather uneven and the lack of rain over the previous fortnight had made it a little crumblier than one might have wished. Suddenly a ball rose off a good length and hit Geoff on the right thumb — the thumb that was not protected by any padding. Blood poured by the pint from under his thumbnail and poor Geoff had to come off, bravely hiding his agony and staunching the flow of best Group O Rhesus Positive by sticking his thumb in his mouth. If ever there was a moment that called for sympathy, this was it. His mother looked up from her knitting and saw her six-foot, sixteen-stone elder son walking forlornly back from the scene of the carnage. Did she rush to his side, and with a mother's practised hand set about repairing the damage? No. She looked at him and said in a voice that rang across the ground, 'Seeing you like that takes me right back to when you were a boy. Do you remember? You were eleven or twelve before you gave up sucking your thumb, and that little teddy bear you used to take to bed with you, what was he called? Oh yes, Skiddy-Poo, that was it. You didn't sleep well unless he was with you until you were fifteen or so. Oh yes, a regular little suck-a-thumb you were.'

Geoff never invited his mother to another cricket match. His thumb healed completely, but his confidence never lost the scar. By the end of the next season, his batting average was back into single figures, a statistic that may owe something to the standard greeting of all opposing captains as he began his innings: 'Hi there, Skiddy-Poo! How's the thumb today? Still tasting good, I hope.'

All the Compleat Cricketer asks for is sympathy. Sincerity can wait.

To conclude, a brief word about hooliganism. This is evolving into a diurnally augmenting sociological implications situation in all sectors of our ongoingly materialistic society. Cricket is not excluded. Hooliganism in cricket, as in association football and other professional sporting pastimes, is the responsibility of the spectator. We all have a moral duty to stamp out hooliganism, to deal a heavy and vicious blow against those who wish to intimidate by force the peace-loving majority. However it is worth differentiating between mindless violence, which must be kicked in the groin whenever it is encountered, and harmless fun, which is a normal part of all public activity.

When I say harmless fun, I am referring to such innocent japes as attacking the opposing captain with a stump or filling the visiting wicket-keeper's box with superglue. Putting bromide into the other side's tea pot or felling their opening bowler with a well-aimed sausage roll are further examples of simple practical jokes to which nobody can take offence, and none but a stickler for the rules of etiquette would attempt to limit such boisterousness. These activities can, however, be starkly contrasted with major acts of brutish hooliganism like laughing at my jumble sale flannels or signalling my well-disguised slower ball as a wide. Such blatant pieces of anti-social hooliganism will inevitably incur the public wrath of all those who love and protect the ethos of this noble game.

*   *   *

Have you noticed how, at some stage, in any game, most of the people there go for a walk around the pitch? The players do it, usually when they are out for a lower score than they believe their skills deserve (i.e. every time they bat) in order to work off some of the anger they feel at this latest injustice of life. The wives and girlfriends do it, probably in order to compare notes discreetly on the relative merits of their Compleat Cricketers, and in some cases to argue energetically when both discover they are laying claim to the same person. The little children do it, cutting corners from silly mid-on to fly-slip as they go in order to get to the stagnant pond/bramble patch/dead pheasant which is today's major attraction. The amazing fact is that they all do it anti-clockwise. For some reason everyone who walks round a cricket pitch in Britain does so in the opposite direction from the way the bathwater swirls down the plug-hole. Why? What deep mysteries of gravity, magnetism and cricket does this phenomenon point to? I have heard from those Australians of my acquaintance who take baths that Down Under the water gurgles out anti-clockwise, for typical bloody-minded Australian reasons, no doubt. Does this mean that people walk round cricket pitches clockwise in Australia? I do not know. All I know is that whereas answers to most of the spectatorial problems of our time can be found, and have been provided in these past few pages, this must be the subject of further research — yet another good reason to carry on striving to be the Compleat Spectator.

8
FITNESS AND YOU

Cricket is, as you might possibly have gathered by now, not only a sport but also an athletic pursuit. Which means you have to be at your optimum fitness to succeed. I am sorry to have to break this news to you at such a late stage in this book, and I suppose it is possible that some people who have come this far may well feel that now they can go no farther. Now is the time to abandon hope of ever being a successful cricketer. But pray do not hurl this book at the cat in disgust, do not go out and buy *The Compleat Sheep Dog Triallist*. Bear with me a moment or two longer.

Playing cricket is not like playing football, rugby or lacrosse. It does not involve incessant running, fighting and hacking like those other pastimes I have just mentioned. It is taken at a more gentle pace and optimum fitness for cricket does not imply the ability to give Sebastian Coe ten yards start and still lap him in the mile. Optimum fitness in many cases means the ability to hold oneself in an upright position at the start of the match. Optimum fitness means the ability to fit into last seasons's flannels without cutting off the blood supply to all parts of the anatomy below the belt. Colin Cowdrey was invalided out of the RAF with flat feet, but he then went on to play 114 Tests for England. I know many a stalwart of the local club sides who has been invalided out of the Star and Garter flat on his back at closing time, and who has gone on to drop 114 catches at second slip the following day. Cricket fitness is, thank heavens, not a matter of press-ups and twice-weekly games of squash. It is the art of tailoring your physical shortcomings to the needs of the team.

None of us are perfect. Some are more perfect than others, admittedly, and some of us are really rather repulsive. All the

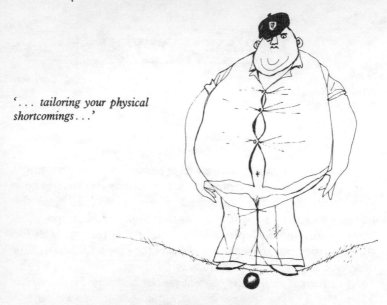

'... *tailoring your physical shortcomings*...'

same, we all have some deficiencies of which you will be painfully aware by now, having gazed fondly at yourself in the bathroom mirror as recommended in Chapter 2. You have two options in seeking to overcome the dampening effects of these howling errors in Nature's attempts to shape your body athletically. One is to submit yourself to a regime of strict dietary control and planned exercise, to bring about a reshaping of the body so total that even your mother won't recognise you, and young ladies will hurl themselves at you in the street, with cries of 'Take me now, you perfect specimen of manhood'. (If this happens, you had better hope your wife won't recognise you, either.) We will consider this option later. The other option, far more difficult to achieve and therefore the one we must face up to first, is that of disguising your failings so that your captain and, more important-ly, the opposition, are not aware of any slight physical defect in your make-up. This requires a triumph of mind over matter, an outbreak of mass hysteria among players and spectators alike such has not been seen since the Gadarene Swine plunged mindlessly into oblivion two millennia ago. It goes without saying, therefore,

'... *this man has Dedication*...'

that disguising your physical condition can be difficult, usually more difficult than curing it. However, injuries and deformities have their uses.

Professional cricketers worry about injuries and do all in their power to avoid having to sit out a match or two. To achieve an injury-free existence, they put themselves through a regimen of running, weightlifting and sessions on the masseur's table which are far more unpleasant and debilitating than any injury short of decapitation. However, this is called Dedication, and it is what cricketers who are getting paid for it need to prove they have. Everybody knows that anybody fool enough to open the bowling in the first match of the season on a grey April afternoon has Dedication. Everybody watching him running into a force 8 gale, stomach bouncing outside last season's flannels, face as red as the Lancashire rose, knows this man has Dedication. His wife, who has to carry him home, soak him for two hours in a hot bath and spray him with two coats of Deep Heat rub, knows as she watches him stiffen up to ferro-concrete levels of hardness that he has Dedication but not enough sense to swat a fly with. At his age he should know better!

Too right, he should. Nobody should volunteer for the willing carthorse slot in the first game of the season. Look what happened to carthorses. They are all but extinct. On the other hand, the first game of the season is a great chance for bowling glory. Batsmen out of practice, suspect wickets, uncricketing weather: all the elements are there for a surprise breakthrough by any man who can turn his arm over higher than Christina Willes of Kent whose crinoline caused the birth of round-arm bowling in 1822. To solve this dilemma between the desire to act and the need not to overdo it, all that is needed is an awareness of the potential problem, so that you can persuade your captain to take you off before the unaccustomed strain of running in and bowling has torn hamstrings asunder and pulled muscles through a hedge backwards. A little bit of subtlety can give you 1 for 12 in three overs and a sympathetic round of applause, instead of 1 for 108 in eleven overs and three weeks in traction. The first thing to do is to make known your Nagging Injury. This is not specifically a reference to the lady wife, although some cricketers of my acquaintance have received the original blow that has graduated over the years into a Nagging Injury through the good offices of their spouses.

The Nagging Injury is the reason why you have to be taken off as soon as their no. 6 comes in and hits three fours in an over off the fellow bowling at the other end. The Nagging Injury is the reason why that sharp chance in the covers didn't quite stick and why you missed the straight one that confronted you second ball. No cricketer is complete without one, and it is up to you to develop one from the moment you are selected for your new team. It is absolutely no good being fit, as fitness eliminates at least three quarters of all known excuses for failure. You must be fit 'on your day', but it is essential that you retain the freedom to decide, retrospectively, whether or not this has been your day.

By far the most popular Nagging Injury is the Bad Back. Let me lay my cards on the table by stating here and now that I suffer from a Bad Back, caused by a motor cycle accident at the age of seventeen. The advantage of a Bad Back is that it is entirely undetectable to the human eye (unless you wish to overdo it to Quasimodo proportions), and coupled with a plausible How It Happened story, it can be allowed to flare up at any moment you like. My How It Happened story is backed up by a yellowing cutting from our local paper, which unfortunately only mentions a broken arm. I also keep a bottle of highly complicated pills in my cricket bag. Nobody has yet discovered they are not pain killers but artificial sweeteners. The disadvantage of the Bad Back is that because everybody says they have one a certain amount of scepticism and derision amongst your team-mates is the usual reaction, rather than the sympathy and concern you were looking for. The other disadvantage of this particular Nagging Injury is that if you really have got a bad back it hurts like no other pain known to man and can cause your downfall on the rare occasions when you wish to carry on playing.

Another popular injury is The Knee. The Nagging Knee, like the Bad Back, is externally indistinguishable from its healthy counterparts, which is good news, and it is fairly easy to collapse in a heap a split second after disaster has struck your cricketing efforts, and to make it look as though the collapse was the cause rather than the effect of the disaster. Most knees also have scars on them from boyhood scrapes, so it is not difficult to suggest that a piece of 1962 school playground which has left its mark on your kneecap is actually the scar from 'an exploratory operation'. What's good enough for Ian Botham is good enough for anybody else. All in all, knees are the perfect answer to the Nagging Injury problem, with one crucial exception. If your local vicar plays for your club, do not opt for The Knee. I recount in this connection the tragic tale of a chap called Henry Sloman, who appeared briefly for our village team a few years back. Henry was a promising cricketer with all the right attributes when he selected our club as the medium for exercising his cricketing talents. He had all the Kit, including optional fore-arm protector. His wife volunteered to make the teas and his 13-year-old son did the scoring with eagerness. Henry walked out to bat with a genuine Gary Sobers forward lope and in his third game for us he even scored two runs. His career was well set. In his fourth game, he dropped a sitter at mid-on. Most of us would have immediately claimed the sun was in our eyes, unquestionably the supreme cricket excuse. But not Henry. His left leg buckled underneath him and he was heard to yell, 'It's the knee again'. The Rev. Tony Thomas, fielding at first slip, looked at him but said nothing.

At tea (provided by Mrs Sloman, including ginger snaps and clotted cream scones), Rev. Tony asked Henry how long the knee had been troubling him.

'Well,' said Henry, wondering how much he could get away with, 'it's an old Rugby injury from my schooldays.' So far so good.

'Which knee is it?' asked Tony sympathetically.

'The right one,' replied Henry, rolling up his left trouser leg. A brief pause ensued, during which knowing glances were exchanged.

The Rev. Thomas moved his accent up a gear into Ecclesiastical Welsh, which we all recognised as a clear warning sign, and spoke as he peered closely at both Henry's knees (just to make sure, look you).

'Do you know,' he said, as though searching for the significance of his text for next Sunday's sermon, 'I have judged simply hundreds of Knobbly Knee competitions in church fetes and bazaars up and down the country, and I think I know a thing or two about knees by now.'

Henry went white, although there was no indication that it was the pressure of the vicar's finger on his patella that precipitated the change in colour.

'It looks to me like you've got two very sound knees there, Henry,' continued the Rev. 'Not like Jim here, who's just taken 8 for 31 off his long run. He's got a really strange left knee.'

'Would've been 9 for 31 if you'd held that bloody catch,' muttered Jim through a mouthful of cucumber sandwich.

'It's a funny thing about knees,' said Henry weakly. 'They can get better just as quickly as they get worse.'

No more was said, but Henry never volunteered his services again for us after that fateful afternoon. Two weeks later, Jim asked Rev. Thomas to look at his left knee, 'seeing as you're such an expert, like.'

'Don't know the first thing about them, Jim. They all look the same to me.'

'But vicar, you knew all about knees when Sloman was playing for us the other week. You called his bluff all right.'

'He might have two tin knees for all I can tell, but the thing is, Jim, I didn't really take to Mr Sloman. He left a fly-button in the collection the other Sunday, so I knew he wasn't the type we needed in the eleven.'

You have been warned.

The purpose of the Nagging Injury is simply to allow you to time your withdrawal from the front line of cricketing activity, rather than to act as a full blown excuse for failure. Excuses must be far more varied and imaginative than a Nagging Injury, which is by definition incurable. If your failures are incurable, then there is a serious risk that you might eventually be dropped (O tell it not in Gath, publish it not in Askelon). No team wants a player who is inevitably bound to fail, but somebody who has to be nursed through a slightly tricky physical condition and who can sometimes bring out the best in himself in spite of adversity — now there is a pillar of the side.

If you are really looking for Fitness (note the capital F), then I cannot for one minute imagine why you have read this far. You have got hold of the wrong book altogether. Fitness requires Exercise, and this is something that I cannot in all honesty recommend to anybody who really wants to succeed at cricket. The trouble is that your new super fit body will not necessarily house a better cricketer than the present rather seedy, overblown version that the local punters all know and love. All exercise will do is give you further opportunities to acquire debilitating injuries. However, for those of you who feel cheated if a sporting manual does not contain full and explicit details of the way

Canadian paratroopers prepare for a Saturday night out in Medicine Hat, I will compromise and give details of a few Compleat Exercises for the Successful Cricketer.

1) *Jogging*. Jogging helps build up speed and stamina. The Compleat Cricketer needs speed and stamina for a number of reasons, e.g. avoiding being run out by anybody in your team who has a lower batting average than you (if such a body exists). Speed is essential, also, for disappearing rapidly when volunteers are called upon to umpire/score/put up the sightscreen/mark out the pitch (perm any two of four). Jogging helps. The Compleat Cricketer jogs every morning from bedroom to bathroom and back. If this is too much at first, try jogging one way first, and, if even this is too difficult, just jog out of bed twice a week.

2) *Trunk Curls*. Trunk Curls are a very valuable exercise for reducing the waistline, strengthening the stomach muscles and generally shaping up which is necessary if you are to struggle into last season's flannels... However, if you are too large around the middle and suffer from weak stomach muscles, then the problem with trunk curls is that they are DIFFICULT. No only that, if you manage to do one, it HURTS. Probably the best answer is to watch somebody else doing them, and imagine how much good it would be doing for you if only it was your sort of exercise. Then tear last season's flannels on a nail and have to go out and buy a new pair.

3) *Arms Bend*. A strong pair of arms are very necessary for throwing, bowling and arguing with the umpire. A little bit of gentle weight-lifting will strengthen the upper arms to such an extent that you will certainly need to replace that old cricket shirt, which anyway seems to have shrunk around the central portion. Go to the pub, every night if you are strongly committed to the health kick, and order a pint of mine host's best. By lifting the glass regularly from bar to lips and back, you will quickly develop the sort of biceps rarely seen on a sportsman.

4) *Skipping*. Strongly recommended. Skipping all exercise is the most sensible course.

The other aspect of Fitness is Diet. A quick stroll down to your local bookshop (provided it is not too far: too long a stroll smacks

'. . . *all diet books have one basic fault . . .*'

of exercise) will give you the opportunity to look at all the diet books on sale. There are simply hundreds. Diet books are probably the only things that outnumber exercise books (the Jane Fonda type, not the Form 3B type) on the shelves. Dieting is big business, and clearly the easiest way to lose weight is to buy every diet book that hits the shops, as this will leave you with no money to spend on food. However, for the Compleat Cricketer, all diet books have one basic fault. They do not advocate participation in the Cricket Tea. However, as we all know, tea is the Alpha and the Omega of the Cricketer's Diet, the event around which the game is built. In this chapter, I will dwell a little on this essential aspect of our summer game, partly in order to plug the gaping hole in our understanding and partly in the hope that this chapter will qualify this book for the Diet Book shelves in the bookshop, which is where the bestsellers come from.

There are three types of Cricket Tea, the Smart, the Standard and the Repulsive. Typical menus would be:

1) The Smart Tea. Typical of some Wandering sides — 1 Zingari, The Grannies, The Stragglers etc.

Pimms No. 2

———

Saumon fumé
Salade aux avocats

———

Selection de sandwichs
— Caviare
— Pâté de foie
— Cucumber
— Miel naturel

———

Les scones avec crème et confiture

———

Les gâteaux de Fortnum's et Harrods
tout sticky avec beaucoup d'alcoöl

———

Champagne

(4.15 for 4.30 R.S.V.P.)

2) The Standard Tea. Plain village fare, as consumed twice each weekend in pavilions up and down the country.

Selection de Sandwichs
— Cucumber
— Pâté de poisson
— Oeufs hard-boiled
— Tomate
— Cucumber
— Spam

———

Les gâteaux de chocolat ou de fruit, et quelquechose un peu crumbly et unappetising.

Rolls de Saucisse
_____

Squash d'orange
_____

Thé

(4.45–5.05 pm)

3) The Tea-As-You-Would-Be-Done-By. Gasworks B v. Lower Scoring Sunday XI.

Cucumber Sandwichs
_____

Buns de Rocher
_____

More cucumber sandwichs avec du pain vieux et tout curled-up aux coins
_____

Thé, ou quelque chose dirty et wet.

(4.45–4.46 pm)

Each tea serves a different purpose. The Smart Tea is designed to feed the wives, consorts and offspring of the players rather than the team itself, as the smart wandering sides are the only type of team who consistently bring their own spectators with them, and spectators must be fed. The cost of the Smart Tea starts at a fiver, which is of course small beer for most of the participants in the feed. The Smart Tea will last for as long as is deemed suitable and the cricketers themselves will probably limit their intake to the Pimms and the champagne. It is therefore difficult to assess how significant the Cricket Tea is in maximising the efficiency of the Amateur Cricketer. Is avocado a more significant aid to the spinning finger than rock buns? Does pâté de foie keep bat close to pad more consistently than spam? We must resign ourselves to uncertainty on this matter, which will not discourage the consumption of everything available whenever we are lucky enough to play in a game where the Smart Tea is served.

The Standard Tea is well researched. The basis of it is the

cucumber sandwich and of course the lettuce that pervades everything that cricket has to offer, Lettuce, I am assured, contains a substance called lactucarium, which in times past was used as a substitute for opium in sleeping draughts. Wild lettuce, especially, can have a significant soporific effect when consumed in large quantities. Feed enough of it to the opposition, and your team's prospects of victory are greatly enhanced. Feed it to the spectators and they will not be awake to notice your brief innings or 0 for 92. Feed it to your captain, and with any luck he will not remember your appalling performances next time the selection committee meets.

Lettuce is not the only chemically-active ingredient of the Standard Tea. Tea itself contains caffeine, which will be enough of a stimulant to counteract the drugged lettuce. The carbohydrates in the bread, scones and cakes will also energise the Compleat Cricketer, unless he eats a Compleat Plateful, in which case the extra weight taken on board may cause problems in the nimbleness department. Eggs are of course full of virtually every vitamin, stimulant, depressant and cholesterol, as well as being very good for coagulating the digestion after the mouthfuls of fish paste, spam and sausage rolls of unknown recipe that give a sinister meaning to the phrase 'rapid movements in the post-tea session.'

The Standard Tea costs 70p these days, plus a further 50p contribution to the club raffle. The third type of tea is best avoided. Bring your own, steal somebody else's, don't eat anything at all, but whatever you do, steer clear of the rock buns. A tea that consists almost entirely of rock buns and a brown liquid that would contravene the Trade Descriptions Act if it were described as tea is not to be tasted. The rock buns (starch, cholesterol and currants) will do wonders for your energy and will unquestionably give you a second wind (and almost certainly a third and a fourth, much to the disgruntlement of anybody fielding within range of you). They will also break your teeth more effectively than a bouncer from Malcolm Marshall, and not even the high corrosive power of the 'tea' itself can reduce these chunks of granite to comfortably digestible pieces.

The point of the Cricket Tea is not so much what you consume, but what you can persuade others to consume. If you have been fielding before tea, watching the opposition pile on the runs at a rate of six an over, most of which have passed through your legs or beyond the reach of your folded arms, you will have noticed their massively built no. 7 who is obviously their opening bowler. Your duty is plain — he must be over-exposed to the tea menu, so that the extra weight taken on board slows him down even more than your umpire's early call of 'Wide,' which always involves an arm swung sideways into the bowler as he delivers the ball (see Chapter 6). Persuade him to eat the entire plate of wild lettuce, and stand clear as the lactucarium takes effect. I have never seen a sixteen-stone fast bowler overcome by wild lettuce, but I imagine the event is similar to a bull elephant being shot by a tranquillising dart. Make sure their no. 7 is the opening bowler, though. It is pointless drugging their third man and long on to the eyeballs, only to find your side skittled out by the slim nineteen-year-old with glasses who is high on two spoonfuls of sugar in his three-bagged tea.

If you have been batting before tea and the match isn't over yet, the obvious solution to the problem of how to ensure your opponents do not surpass your total before the pubs open is in the tea itself, the drink not the meal. It is a well-documented fact that airline pilots are encouraged to drink tea rather than coffee on long intercontinental flights. Both drinks are warm and brown, both are rich in caffeine, so why do the pilots have to drink tea? The answer is that tea goes through the system far more completely than coffee and it is vital for the long-term health of airline captains, who sit uncomfortably for hours on end with nothing but a few dials to look at and a joystick to hold on to, that their kidneys function successfully and often. Tea helps, coffee doesn't.

So what will happen to a batsman who has drunk six cups of tea a few minutes before going out to bat? Before he is into double figures, his concentration will begin to wander, his stance will become cross-legged and fidgety, and with any luck the first speculative lbw appeal will have him racing for the pavilion without waiting to see whether or not he was given out. 'Retired' will be the entry in the scorebook, but the result is the same: once again our side is in with a chance.

Apart from the Tea Ceremony, there is one other main source of alimentary refreshment partaken by the Compleat Cricketer, which can have a significant effect on his performance on the field. I refer to the pub. Visits to the pub, which is inevitably extremely close at hand, can take place either before or after the game, or more commonly both. The visit before the match, usually to eat a packet of cheese and onion crisps in lieu of lunch, can lead to the same kind of problems as those caused by tea, viz. a need to retire behind the pavilion at regular intervals. It can also improve the standard of cricket quite significantly. I once played in a game where our captain, in a spirit of generosity rare among visiting teams, matched drink for drink the entire home team in the pub at lunchtime. Those of us who remained sober consoled

'... 22 yards of ale...'

ourselves with the fact that at least our captain would have no memory of the game, and that therefore our incompetences would go unpunished as far as future selection committees were concerned. What we had failed to take into account was the state of the wicket, which resembled an assault course for Centurion tanks. The ball moved yards each way and reared up off a length for even the flimsiest of bowlers, and within minutes we were reduced to 30-odd for 6. At this point our captain was helped into his pads and box, pointed in the general direction of the action and given a shove. Thanks to his massive alcoholic intake, he saw three balls where the rest of us saw but one, and was always able to hit the right one with one of his three bats. By the time he fell onto his stumps and had to be carried back to the pavilion, he had made 40, and our score finished at just below the 100 mark, which on that wicket proved to be a very respectable score. Generally speaking though, unless you wish each game to be but a blur in your memory, drinking 22 yards of ale before the match is inadvisable.

Drinking after the match is expensive but unavoidable. It can be especially expensive for any member of either side who has hit a 50 or taken 5 wickets, as they are expected to buy a round to celebrate. There is a considerable art to letting the final four slip between your hands to complete a 50, or making sure you are bowled by a fellow who has already taken 4 wickets. That way you ensure yourself a free drink afterwards. If ever you should find yourself in the position of having taken 4 wickets with 3 left to fall, or at 47 not out with twelve overs left to play, all you need to do to avoid having to fork out a vast sum on beer (at present about three times as expensive as four-star petrol) is to give rein to the Nagging Injury. Which takes us back to the beginning again.

The Naughty Bits

There has been considerable controversy about whether or not a healthy sex life is compatible with a healthy sporting life and many would argue that regular sports participation does wonders for your more intimate physical endeavours. The unanswered question, however, is Does Sex Interfere With Cricket? I am not only referring to a quick grope with the village policeman's nineteen-year-old daughter behind the sightscreen, which clearly does interfere with cricket unless undertaken between overs (she's doing the teas, remember, so she'll be busy then). I am alluding to the more metaphysical question, Is Sexual Prowess Compatible With Sporting Brilliance? To put it on a more recognisable plane, Is Sexual Adequacy Compatible With Any Cricketing Success Whatsoever? I fear the answer is no.

Lord Olivier, in his autobiography, wrote that 'the most magnificent specimens in almost every branch of athletic sport prove to be disappointing upon the removal of that revered jockstrap.' Leaving aside the fact that the vast majority of cricketing jockstraps have never before shared the same sentence as the word 'revered,' it appears that the Compleat Cricketer cannot expect also to be the Compleat Stud. Pillow and willow are incompatible.

There is one problem that must be addressed in attempting to moderate the bodily passions in the interests of cricket, and that is that Compleat Cricketers are extraordinarily attractive to people of the opposite gender. Maybe it is the sight of the fore-arm protector set at a rakish angle, maybe it is the expanse of gut ballooning out beyond the confines of shirt and flannels, maybe it is the subtle aroma of linseed oil and last week's socks. Whatever it is, women find it hard to keep their hands to themselves when cricketers are in the offing. The obstacles to be overcome in the pursuit of cricketing perfection are manifold. But we must be strong.

Do not think for one minute that I am advocating total abstinence, although to do it the way Gandhi did it and test oneself every night by sleeping chastely with nubile eighteen-year-olds might be fun. Total abstinence would result in a spate of divorce cases that would block the courts for years and give the local paper even more reason not to find room for your team's most recent exploits. But abstinence during the season will help your cricket, except for those brief periods when your Nagging

Injury forces you to make yourself unavailable for selection for a couple of weeks.

Look on the bright side. The Joy Of Cricket is much more satisfying than the Joy Of Sex, and anyway it goes on for four or five hours at a time. So go to it, dear reader, or rather don't go to it.

Now that you know how to achieve optimum cricket fitness, it is time to look at where to put this new found glow in the cheeks to good use. The bright eyes, the Nagging Injury and the bulging chequebook can all be tried and tested — on tour.

9
THE GRAND TOUR

Sunday July 15

1900 Another close run game for High Dudgeon, losing in the last over (before tea) by nine wickets. This disaster has not diverted our attention from the main objective for the day, choosing the team for our tour of Cornwall at the end of next month. The selection committee settles into the snug at The Ploughman's Arms to pick the team. There's Dave Hodges, our captain, sitting next to Bert Robinson, who is well into his fourth pint by now. Jock Patel is sitting on his wallet as usual and then there's me. It's Jock's round. This could be a long evening.

The highlight of any cricketer's season is the Tour. For some, selection to tour means a winter in Australia or the West Indies. A little lower down the scale, county cricketers will spend ten days at a time on the road, visiting all the exciting parts of Britain like Buxton, Chelmsford and Guildford. For a Cambridge or Oxford undergraduate, selection for the pre-University match tour is an important stepping stone in his cricket career, while down at the bottom of the cricketing skills ladder, where you and I play, the Tour gives even a poor cricketer the chance to be thrown out of a completely new selection of pubs somewhere miles away from anywhere he's played before. This is an opportunity that should not be passed by.

Even from a cricketing point of view, the tour represents a chance that must be grabbed at as eagerly as if it were the barmaid at the Dog and Duck in Lostwithiel. For the junior members of an England touring party, it provides a chance to watch the best players in England (plus one or two from South Africa and the West Indies) at close quarters for three or four months, and thus

'. . . the highlight of any cricketer's season . . .'

pick up a few pointers to improving your game. For the county cricketer motoring around Britain, the tour is the period when you can renew your acquaintance with the landladies of Buxton, Chelmsford, Guildford etc. who were so kind and thoughtful to you last year. You may even find the sock that went missing on Thursday 8 July 1982. But the reason I go on tour each year is to work my way up the club averages.

2330 The selection process grinds on. All those who are taking their family holiday in August just because that is when the schools are out have been ruled out, so we are as so often limited to the very young and the very old. This is what makes the tour such an attraction to me. We always lose in Cornwall. All touring teams lose, and we are never a team to go against tradition. Me, I put it down to homesickness. The plight of a man like myself separated, even for only a few days, from the wife and three children under the age of six leads inexorably to alcohol and loose women as I try to overcome the loneliness of enforced separation from a home filled with nappies, broken toys and cries of 'Daddy, I want a drink' at 3.30 am. The bleak touring lifestyle can seriously affect a man's cricketing skills. Even those of us whose cricketing skills are unlikely to be adversely affected by anything short of nuclear holocaust can take heart as we watch our star players like Dave reduced even temporarily to something less than star status. As an added bonus, I am secure in the knowledge that my particular style of batting is as likely to earn me three or four runs in Cornwall as it is in High Dudgeon. If last year is anything to go by, I might even improve.

Bert Robinson, who finally gave up waiting for Jock to buy a round, came back with four refilled glasses and the statement, 'It's the Dog and Duck again this year.'

Bert enjoyed the Dog and Duck last year and the year before, for reasons not unconnected with the physical charms of the barmaid. A change of venue would reduce by one the number of available cricketers for the tour, but Dave confirms that the bookings have been made. 'Let's hope the weather is better than last year, though,' he adds as an afterthought.

Bert thought last year's rain was perfect as it gave him a chance

130

to indulge in a variety of new pub games with the barmaid, but for the rest of us it caused grave problems. The money ran out and we had nothing left to pay for tickets to the local Odeon to see *The Sound Of Music* for the umpteenth time as the rain sheeted down on the Monday afternoon. This year the team must include a plutocrat, somebody with more money than sense.

'William Blenkinsop,' suggested Jock Patel.

'Who's he?'

'He has a lot of money, and wishes to become a member of the cricket club. It would be a very effective idea to invite him to tour with us. I will allow him to share transportation and accommodation with me.'

'Can he play cricket?'

'I am not sure. He wears glasses.'

'So does Geoff Boycott. Let's include this Blenkinsop.'

'Seconded.'

'He's in. Who else?'

Bert Robinson, hon. sec., pulled a crumpled envelope out of his back pocket and placed it neatly in a ring of beer on the table. The list of names became a soggy illegible mess. Bert picked up the envelope again and waved it about in an attempt to dry out the candidates for the touring party. Jock and I were sprayed with inky beer.

'I know "Tights" Royston was on the list,' mumbled Bert apologetically.

'The lobster must be good again this year. I hear he's discovered three more little restaurants in the area which he hopes to try between games.'

'Nigel McGee says he'll be back from his Abu Dhabi trip the day before so he's on for the tour.'

'Gerry Gable's agent phoned and said that Gerry would be resting between engagements that week, and provided that nothing major cropped up, he'd be coming. His agent called it "a welcome break in a busy year". Those two episodes of *Emmerdale Farm* and a floor polish ad voiceover obviously constitute a busy year for our favourite Oscar nominee.'

'There's Hampson, Baker and Brown. Tony Hampson told me

this afternoon, just after he dropped that catch, that all three of them would be O.K. to tour.'

'Well that gives us the hooligan element, anyway.'

'And a wicket-keeper.'

'Bob Harcourt-Fanshawe is back from the grouse moors by then, so he'll come too. And Ken Jones tells me his boy Peter wants to come along.'

'How old is he?'

'Fifteen, I think.'

'Is he any good?'

'Are you any good?'

So the touring party is assembled. Thirteen names for three games at the end of August. The preparation is now almost complete.

Wednesday August 8

2215 Need to cultivate the Nagging Injury in time for the tour. Require to give the impression that my usual 2 or less is caused by fitness problem not by complete lack of talent. Have been reading interesting work about the poet Keats, who in most respects comes out as a bit of a weed. However in March 1819 he wrote that 'Yesterday I got a black eye whilst taking up a cricket bat. Brown, a friend in disaster, applied a leech to my eyelid and there is no inflammation this morning.' This looks like the sort of injury I need, as it will not prevent the injured party (me) from joining in the after-match festivities, but it will rationalise my ineffectiveness on the greensward. Incidentally, this letter of Keats' would seem to be the first literary reference to F.R. 'Heart Like A Lettuce' Brown, of Surrey, Northants and England. Could it also be that the leech referred to is none other than T.E. 'Barnacle' Bailey?

Mature reflection leads me to consider that hitting myself with a cricket bat might hurt. Hope Gerry Gable brings his make-up with him, then I can black my eye without the pain usually connected with said operation.

Thursday August 30

0930 Entire party assembles at the High Dudgeon pavilion, except for those who have made separate travel arrangements. This means four of us are on hand to transport the kit to Cornwall, and of these four only I have a car, and a Ford Cortina 1.6 GLE at that. My fellow travellers are the newcomer, this William Blenkinsop, who looks remarkably unathletic even by High Dudgeon standards; Jock Patel, who has lived up to his promise to share transportation with Mr Blenkinsop; and young Peter Jones, who is spending the last few days of the school holidays on tour with us, much to the relief of his parents. It seems only yesterday that his mother, the luscious and well-built Mrs Jones (née Dawn Sidebottom, the darling of 4C) was wheeling young Peter in his pram behind the bowler's arm every Sunday, but it must be all of fourteen years ago now.

1030 We have not gone thirty miles when an argument breaks out between Blenkinsop, seated comfortably in the front passenger seat, and young Peter, who is largely hidden on the back seat next to the well-built Jock Patel and underneath pads, bats, gloves and shrimping nets that did not fit in the boot. The argument is over whether the driving test is more difficult than Maths 'O' Level. It is resolved when Blenkinsop declares that more people are killed taking the driving test than during Maths 'O' Level, to which Peter replies that more people pass the driving test, so Maths 'O' Level must be harder. I suspect that young Jones is speaking from bitter experience. Blenkinsop is beginning to get on my nerves. Why was he picked if all he can do is peer through his pebble glasses and argue over the most unimportant subjects with a fifteen-year-old boy?

1130 Stop for petrol. Blenkinsop pays.

1245 Stop for lunch. Blenkinsop pays. I think I now understand why he was selected. Good old William, say I.

1840 Arrive at the Dog And Duck. Three others of the team have arrived before us, but that is only because they have been holidaying with 'friends in the area'. In the case of Bob Harcourt-Fanshawe, that means the landed gentry, but as far as Bert

Robinson is concerned, it means the barmaid at the Dog And Duck. He tells his wife every year that the tour lasts for two weeks, and he also tells her that the pub is called the 'Landlady's Arms', so that she can't say he didn't tell her he sleeps in the landlady's arms. If it wasn't for the fact that our milkman takes his holiday in the same two weeks as Bert, but there are always plentiful supplies of milk, butter and eggs in the fridge when Bert gets back, I'd think Bert's wife was a little slow to catch on.

2300   By now the pubs are closing all over the country, and most of the elite High Dudgeon squad have clocked in at the Dog And Duck. Nigel McGee, Export Sales Manager for the local ladies' undergarments company, has telephoned from Heathrow to say he has arrived back successfully from Abu Dhabi, and will be on the 1920 Flymo Airways to somewhere within fifty miles of our pub. Opening bowler Mark Brown bent his car failing to notice the corner at the bottom of the lane not fifty yards from the Dog And Duck, but he always hits something on tour and it is rarely the stumps. The forces are gathering for the battle.

Friday August 31

0830   Am awakened by a hammering on the front door of the pub. It is Nigel McGee, whose journey from the local airport to our GHQ has taken longer than his journey from Abu Dhabi to London. The problem was that he did not know where he had landed, and the taxi driver did not know where he was going. McGee, looking rather more haggard than a traveller in ladies' knickers ought to look, is concerned about how to hide this massive taxi bill in his expenses. The problem is solved by that first-class chap Bill Blenkinsop, who emerges in a silk dressing gown and pays the taxi driver.

0945   The team assembles for breakfast. 'Tights' Royston, our permanent gourmet, is already well into a second plate of sausages, tomatoes, fried eggs and bacon, which in his opinion will only go to waste if somebody doesn't eat it. 'Don't want to upset mine host on the first morning, do we?' he comments to nobody in particular. Next to him sits Jock Patel, who avoids

134

spending money with the same consummate ease with which he runs out his partners every Saturday and Sunday. He is looking at his fried egg and bacon with limited enthusiasm.

Our three young men about town, Hampson, Baker and Brown, have so far failed to surface, but we know their beds are occupied by at least one person per bed. The team's resident superstar, Gerry Gable, late of *Emmerdale Farm*, a.k.a. Jack Fluck, is not yet down either, but from the state of the bathroom when I moved in to perform the morning ablutions, I can tell he is almost ready to make his grand entrance. The combination of talcum powder, aftershave and other morning smells that pervaded the bathroom was such that I might have smelt rather better unwashed than after ten minutes in that atmosphere.

1100 Team talk. Captain Dave gathers the entire company together to discuss the match this afternoon against St Polpentre, which last year we lost by six wickets. A quick head count shows that somebody is missing, and a recount by Peter Jones, failed Maths 'O' Level and all, confirms that while there should be thirteen honest men and true gathered in hearty good fellowship, we are actually only twelve. 'Where's Bob?' is the cry, for it is our only proficient cricketer and socially acceptable team member, Harcourt-Fanshawe, who is missing. Tony Hampson departs to look for him, and returns three minutes later with the news that the missing man is lying in bed covered in spots.

Cue for loud laughter and ribald comments. 'What a foul disease.' 'Never mind, we'll get them in shingles.' 'I thought Bob only caught the social diseases' etc etc. Sympathy is available only in very small doses. Our captain takes the news to heart.

'So we are down to twelve men,' he says, having passed Maths 'O' Level.

'Eleven men and Gerry,' says an unidentifiable voice at the back.

'What do you mean by that?' asks Equity's favourite son, uncrossing his legs and adjusting the crease in his trousers.

Dave Hodges returns to the subject. 'Peter, do you mind standing down for this one, and I promise you'll play both the other two.' Young Jones doesn't mind. St Polpentre are the strongest of the three teams we are up against, and he knew he'd miss one game anyhow.

'I'll score,' he volunteers.

'Well, we may not need you to,' replies his captain, strangely unenthusiastic about this selfless offer.

'Let's get going,' booms the confident voice of 'Tights' Royston. 'There's a nice little pub in St Polpentre that usually has wonderful lobsters.'

The party sets out, although nobody volunteers to be driven by Mark Brown.

1400 The match begins. The ground is set amidst rolling Cornish hills, with a fresh sea breeze from the pavilion end bringing the cries of the gulls and the roar of the waves to the cricketers ready for battle. It is an idyllic setting in which to lose the toss. We bat first.

Young Peter, having been dissuaded from scoring, insists on umpiring. Steve Baker and Bert Robinson set out to open the innings with all the confidence of Captain Oates walking out into the blizzard.

1530 All out 74. Robinson 19, Hodges 17, Hampson 12 and all the rest got twos and threes or less. Blenkinsop confirmed the earlier impression that sports are clearly not what he is best at, while Gerry Gable looked very debonair making his one run. He is one of the few cricketers I know who plays in a corset, but such is his concern for his public image that he would probably not cover up his face with a helmet even if he were to open the innings against Holding and Marshall. He was more disappointed this afternoon by the lack of autograph-hunters than by his lack of runs. The leading wicket takers were Jock Patel, whose deadly call of 'Yes – No – Oh my goodness' accounted for three of our number, and young Peter, who gave two lbws, one stumped and one caught behind of doubtful veracity. St Polpentre were already talking of making him Man of the Match.

1700 Nigel McGee falls asleep during tea, with the score showing St Polpentre needing another 35 to win with 7 wickets in hand. Jet lag has caught up with him, even if the rock buns haven't. The local captain insists he be allowed to sleep on, and that Peter Jones gives up umpiring and fields as twelfth man. It seems unlikely, after the lbw decision against their opener, that Peter will be Man of the Match after all.

1800 St Polpentre win by six wickets, yet again. The teams retire to the pub, all except McGee, who sleeps happily on.

Saturday September 1

0845 Gerry Gable has beaten me to the bathroom again. Damn! I wade ankle deep through pomade, mouthwash and deodorant to get to the basin. Gable has appeared in two episodes of *Emmerdale Farm* before being written out in a combine harvester tragedy, and he once ordered half a pint of lager in the Rover's Return in an episode of *Coronation Street* originally shown in September 1971. Since then, his original incarnation as Jack Fluck, whose father and grandfather before him ran the village butcher's shop,

'... *Equity's favourite son*...'

has been replaced by the adored superstar Gerry Gable, whose startling appearances as the juvenile lead in the repertory theatres of the country have carved their own niche in theatrical history. As a batsman and desperation change bowler, his career has been scarcely more spectacular. The cricketing equivalent of his *Emmerdale Farm* appearances was surely his 19 not out against Lower Scoring some years ago, when they turned out only nine men and we made 208 for 3 in 34 overs. He is not expected to make a major contribution on tour.

0915 'Tights' Royston has eaten my breakfast. He has also eaten Bill Blenkinsop's, Nigel McGee's and Bob Harcourt-Fanshawe's. I therefore eat Jock Patel's. He seems duly grateful.

0930 Bob is still covered in spots. Nigel McGee is missing. Bert Robinson has lipstick stains on his cricket boots. We look confidently ahead to this afternoon's game.

1000 'Where is Nigel?' asks the skipper.

'He wasn't with us last night,' says Steve Baker, looking a little less athletic than the day before.

'Nor were you after the fourth pint.'

'Enough of that. Who last saw McGee?'

'He was asleep in the pavilion at St Polpentre when I last saw him,' said young Peter.

1215 Mercy dash to the St Polpentre pavilion completed. We are greeted by hammerings on the door and cries of 'Let me out'. Nigel has evidently not strayed far from where we last saw him. Within minutes a touching reunion is effected.

1220 A quick look at the map shows that we are 25 miles from the ground where play is due to start at 1330, and we have no idea where the pub chosen to provide us with lunch might be. Things are looking rough, though not as rough as Nigel McGee, and I turn to Gerry Gable, in whose car we have come.

'What do you think?'

'I think I'm the one standing down this afternoon,' says Gerry. 'I think I'll head to the beach and deepen my already reasonable suntan. It's a bit patchy on the back of my legs.'

'But the beach is in the other direction,' points out McGee.

'I'll phone for someone to pick you up when I get to the beach,' suggests Gerry thoughtfully. McGee threatens to break him into spoon-size lumps unless he runs us straight away to the match, and eventually Gerry sees the reasonableness of this argument.

1650 Really we need not have bothered. By tea the opposition are 187 for 2 and we don't even have the benefit of Peter's umpiring. Steve Baker, our wicket-keeper, is so hung over that extras have already been clapped for their half-century, and 'Tights' Royston, standing immovably at gully for over after over, has dropped three sitters off Tony Hampson, who is not pleased. Still, the sun is shining and Bill Blenkinsop has paid for the teas, so there's not much wrong with our world.

1920 Despite my chanceless 3, and Dave Hodges' 57, we still lose by 62 runs. Peter Jones earned the undying gratitude of his team-mates by running out Jock Patel. The fact that this was our final wicket and it fell with only three balls of the final over remaining in no way diminished our enthusiasm for young Peter's achievement, hitherto considered virtually impossible. 'That boy needs to learn a thing or two about calling,' was Jock's only comment.

2300 The local pub proves to be a very amenable hostelry. After initial bouts of wailing and gnashing of teeth, we shrug off our defeat and drink the local brews in the company of our opponents for several hours. This is the part of the tour which High Dudgeon is good at. Brown, Hampson and Baker run out of money fairly quickly and are reduced to charming the massively-built wench behind the bar into giving them one on the house. Bill Blenkinsop's wallet steps in when the charm fails, which is often.

Sunday September 2

0915 This is our day of rest. I lie back in my bed and gaze about the room. Opposite me, enjoying his first night in a bed for three days, Nigel McGee is scratching himself. On a camp bed by the cupboard Peter Jones is snoring loudly, as he sleeps off the scrumpy of the night before. He looks quite small, but he was very heavy to carry upstairs at 2 o'clock in the morning. McGee stops scratching and throws a shoe at Jones, who does not allow such things to interrupt his sleep.

'What time is it?' asks Nigel.

'Nine-fifteen. The sun's shining, we've no game today and all's well. Except that Gerry's in the bathroom polishing his toupée.'

'Damn.'

0945 'Tights' Royston, ever the democrat, has this morning eaten the breakfasts of Messrs Robinson, Hodges and Gable as well as his own. Jock Patel offers him yet another, which 'Tights' doesn't have the heart to refuse.

'What's everybody doing today, then?'

'Golf. Swimming. Visiting friends in the area. Recovering from chicken-pox. The usual.'

We go our separate ways. I decide to stick close to Bill Blenkinsop, as do Nigel McGee and Jock Patel. Gable is off to make a personal appearance at a church fête, and young Pete is off for a round of golf with Brown, Baker and Hampson. Dave Hodges stays at the Dog And Duck for a while to check the kit and the scorebook before tomorrow's match, which is The Big One. There is optimism that Harcourt-Fanshawe will be fit by then.

'I trust that chicken-pox isn't catching,' says Royston.

'If it is, it's the only thing you will ever catch on a cricket tour,' replies Mark Brown as he loads his golf clubs into the back of Steve Baker's car.

1900 The lads straggle back after their day off. Gerry Gable has signed two autographs, so is well pleased. 'Tights' Royston got the last portion of Beef Wellington and a most exciting strawberry feuilleté at a marvellous restaurant he'd heard so much about and had always wanted to try, and Peter Jones only lost five golf balls. We have been down to the beach and swum a little, but it was cold and McGee said it would give him pneumonia after the heat of Abu Dhabi. Blenkinsop paid for lunch and finished the *Times* crossword while we had our coffee.

0230 A night in at the Dog And Duck is never very quiet. Jock Patel wants to watch television, but 'Tights' organises a darts tournament instead. The first three matches take over an hour because nobody can throw a double when they need one, so everybody gets bored with that and happily agrees that 'Tights' has won. At this point Harcourt-Fanshawe appears like some friendly family ghost in his monogrammed nightshirt at the top of the stairs and announces that he can't sleep with all that racket. The place goes quiet, apart from mumbled phrases like 'Sorry, Bob,' and 'How's the pox?' Bob then strides down the stairs and across to the piano, sits down and begins to belt out *Chattanooga Choo Choo*.

'I didn't really want to sleep anyway,' he says as he switches into *Memories Are Made Of This*. Jock Patel gives up trying to watch television, and even Gerry Gable shuffles elegantly over to the piano to add his ready tenor to the assembled voices. By the time we have run through another three or four favourite oldies (Gerry Gable protesting that he is too young to remember the words), two young ladies have attached themselves to the arms of the pianist, despite dire warnings about his disease-ridden state from his chivalrous fellow cricketers. Bob's activities at the piano make it clear that chicken-pox is a thing of the past. The songs roll on — *She Loves You, My Way, California Here I Come* and even *Sukiyaki*, the Japanese words to which Nigel learnt during one exhaustive sales mission to Tokyo. Jock Patel retires to bed and at 0200 Bert Robinson appears in his dressing gown on the same balcony that had so theatrically yielded Bob to the assembled multitude a few hours earlier.

'Can't a man get any rest in this place?' he shouts. 'The whole pub is vibrating.'

'Well, tell your young lady you've had enough, then.'

By about 0345 we are all in bed. 'Tights' Royston wishes me goodnight as I go into my room. 'The darts tournament went well, don't you think? We must do it again next year.'

Monday September 3

0800 The day of the big match dawns. The team sleeps on, all except me. Just once I want to beat Gerry Gable to the bathroom.

0820 Gerry Gable is in the bathroom, being sick. Mark Brown is in the lavatory, being sick. Steve Baker is in his bedroom, being sick. A mystery virus has struck, and the might of High Dudgeon is laid low.

0810 Jock Patel has chicken-pox. Peter Jones has a hangover. 'Tights' Royston has mild indigestion, which he cures by eating four breakfasts. 'The others won't miss theirs,' he says considerately.

0930 A gathering of the team shows seven fit men, one of whom is 'Tights'. We also have one man probably recovered from chicken-pox, one boy with a hangover and four sick men. Dave Hodges works out his batting order. 'O.K. The two who don't play are Jock and Gerry. We need a wicket-keeper so Steve has to be sobered up, and Mark will have to get better too. Tell them if they want to throw up, to throw up on a length. That will give our bowlers something to aim at.'

My Nagging Injury will have to wait for another day. How did Keats manage to get away with it?

1230 Lunch at some distant pub is a less than festive occasion. Someone has eaten the final lobster, so 'Tights' is reduced to scampi. Steve and Mark are in the car park, breathing deeply and looking even greener and limper than the lettuce in our sandwiches. Peter Jones is drinking orange juice and vowing never to touch alcohol again. Bill Blenkinsop offers to buy a round, but there are no takers.

1400 The match begins. Dave Hodges has not helped matters by losing the toss and being asked to field. Two men are required to buckle on Steve's pads. Mark Brown's opening over is at a slower pace than usual. This is because he has pity on our suffering wicket-keeper, or so he says, but in that case why did he also bowl three wides?

From the other end, Tony Hampson has his own problems.

'Bowler's name!' comes from the pavilion.

'Hampson.'

'Hampton?'

'No, Hampson.'

'Champion?'

'Hampson. Hampson. Oh hell.'

He goes down in the book as 'Patel', and his 4 for 34 ends the season against Jock's name, which goes to show that it pays to check the scorebook very carefully if you hope to clamber above your fellows on the way to the top of the averages. The analysis is Jock's best of the season, made all the more admirable by the state of his health at the time.

1645 Royston, whose only real turn of speed on the cricket pitch is his waddle from gully to pavilion at the start of the tea interval, demolishes single-handedly a plate of cress and cucumber sandwiches, before moving on to the chocolate and strawberry cake. Baker leaves the table hurriedly. Our opponents have made 209 for 9, and sportingly declare.

1900 High Dudgeon all out 129, a state of slight respectability almost entirely due to Bill Blenkinsop, 41 not out. He was almost bowled off his credit cards once, but otherwise snicked and edged his way to a confident career best while all about him were destroyed with appalling regularity. Once again High Dudgeon has completed a clean sweep on its Cornish tour. Played 3 Lost 3.

The kit is loaded into the cars and the long journey home begins.

2330 Somewhere on the M4 we realise we have left Jock Patel and Gerry Gable at the Dog And Duck. Neither of them has a car. In the spirit of true comradeship that is always engendered on our cricket tour, we shrug our shoulders and press on into the night. Jock and Gerry will both find their way back home in time for Sunday's game, and then it will be cricket as usual. Another tour will be just a pile of memories for Saturday night in the pub.

10
RETIREMENT

When I was a young lad, the world was still passing through the Age of the Saturday Matinee. Every Saturday morning, all the children of every neighbourhood would break off from their normal pastimes of letting down car tyres or clacking a stick along the railings in front of the police station, and we would head for the local Odeon, Gaumont or Roxy for another dose of Buck Rogers or The Three Stooges. There were no exceptions to the rule. Every child went every Saturday morning, just as surely as every child hated tapioca pudding or kissing Aunt Martha goodbye. The highlight of these film shows for me was when the heroine, trapped by the villain in a mountain hut or in a crater on the moon, was saved at the last moment by the appearance of our hero. The villain usually shouted at this point, 'Curses, foiled again!' or words to that effect, and as the heroine melted into the hero's arms (this was the soppy bit that was always greeted with catcalls and a shower of sweet-papers and empty ice-cream tubs), one or other would express relief that the heroine had been saved from a Fate Worse Than Death.

The raging question as we left the comfortable, dark and musty atmosphere of the Odeon/Gaumont/Roxy (delete where applicable) and streamed into the Saturday lunchtime sunlight was, 'What fate could be worse than death?' In our single-figure innocence we were unaware of the full significance of the phrase, and various theories were put forward. I remember Fatty Potts, for whom heaven was an unending supply of those strawberry ice lollies you could suck white, suggesting that a fate worse than death would be life without Mrs Gray's sweetshop. Jim 'Cheesefoot' Sanders, whose mother had not yet grasped the basic fact that socks are washable, thought the phrase might refer to having to miss an episode of *Muffin The Mule*, but none of us were willing to make definitive statements on the matter. After all, what fate could be worse than death?

Now I am a man and I know the answer. Retirement from playing cricket is the fate worse than death so regularly referred to by those heroines of yesteryear, a fact that merely confirms how grievously I have ignored the contributions of women cricketers to the game since Ms Christina Willes (see Chapter VIII). They knew, as I now know, that retirement is worse than death, because you are alive to realise your cricket is dead. Retirement is the end of the road all the soldiers in the Second World War were exhorted to keep right on till. Retirement is the answer to Hamlet's problem: to be or not to be. Retirement is being without being, death without death.

Even if a man may not have been much good as a cricketer, retirement hurts. Even if you have never been watched by England selectors or been notified that your name is on the short list for next winter's tour of West Indies, retirement is unappealing. Cricketers can do without it, and most do. Nobody retires just because they are incapable of playing the game with the merest smidgin of skill. Nobody retires just because there is somebody better to take his place in the side. The epitaph of Mrs Sapsea, a character in Charles Dickens' final best-seller *The Mystery Of Edwin Drood*, reads thus: 'Stranger, pause and ask thyself the question, canst thou do likewise? If not, with a blush retire.' If I were to pause after watching Viv Richards hit a century or Abdul Qadir take six wickets and ask myself, Canst thou do likewise, the answer would have to be an emphatic no. But will I therefore with a blush retire? Yet another emphatic no. Without so much as a lowering of the eyes to hide my shame, I will play on until I am carried back to the pavilion in a pine box, because one day before that fate befalls me, I might score a century. One day I might take six wickets, and one day I may be the oldest player since Wilfred Rhodes to play for England.

I hope by now that I have made myself clear. Retirement is not an option. It only occurs when the Compleat Cricketer is forced

'... *nobody retires just because there is somebody better to take his place in the side...*'

into it, when Buck Rogers fails to burst in with his disintegrator gun in the nick of time and save him from the Fate Worse Than Death. Retirement comes in two forms, Temporary and Permanent, and as such differs from Death, which only turns up in the Permanent variety. Temporary retirement is the most popular type, and has two basic causes: Injury and the End of the Season.

Retirement through injury occurs when the Nagging Injury nags more than usual, or a leg is broken falling out of the apple tree. It can last for as long as a couple of months or for as little as one weekend, but just as surely as time brings us all closer to our graves, so also time heals all injuries. What should the Compleat Cricketer do during his period of enforced retirement? Should he sit by the boundary boards, licking his wounds or an ice-cream while his erstwhile team-mates sweat it out on the square? Should he pace up and down like a caged lion deprived of his prey? Should he search out the village policeman's nineteen-year-old daughter to ask her to kiss and/or rub it better?

I would not recommend any of these particular courses of action, as all of them involved making the one basic error that all Temporary Retirees must avoid, to wit turning up at the ground during a match. What you must do, if Injury really does stop play, is to avoid the cricket ground altogether. By all means invite the local constable's daughter to lay her healing hands on you in the privacy of your own home. By all means eat ice-creams in your garden, and do not let me stop you pacing up and down the High Street like the aforementioned unliberated lion. But do not, under any circumstances, let team loyalty persuade you that your presence at the ground to watch your colleagues in action will be of any use to anybody. I trust that by this stage in this treatise, you, dear reader, will anyway long since have dispensed with such outmoded ideas as 'team loyalty'. Cricket is an individual game within a team framework, and the main skills are in shaping the team to benefit you as an individual, and not as some of the more naive and romantic amongst our cricket commentators would have us believe, the other way around. An injured man is as putty in the hands of his able-bodied team-mates. They will use him mercilessly unless he keeps clear of them.

The case of Dale Rossmore is a good example. Dale, a useful opening bowler and aggressive middle-order batsman, broke his leg one spring in a skiing accident. Being a fine team man, he turned up to watch his team's opening game of the season on a cold and blustery April Sunday. As he hobbled up to the pavilion, crutches swinging rhythmically across the muddy turf, he was greeted by a chorus of voices of men he had once considered his friends, making remarks which cast doubts on the seriousness of the injury on show and accusing him of deliberately avoiding selection for the first match of the season against traditionally tough opponents.

Say what you like about young Mr Rossmore, but he will not take insults lightly. After first executing with his left-hand crutch a square cut to the wicket-keeper's stomach, he began berating the captain with a flow of remarks which covered such topics as his own dedication, loyalty and excess of broken limbs, as well as scurrilous rumours regarding the marital status of the parents of several other members of the team. 'I can't help it if I'm injured. I'll be all right in a few weeks.'

'Can you umpire?' asked his captain, timing the strategic question far more sweetly than most of his off drives.

'Yes. Of course I can,' said the foolhardy Dale Rossmore, before he had a chance to regret it. He spent five hours umpiring that day, standing on crutches except when he had to signal four which usually caused him to topple over, slowly but ineluctibly, like a Canadian pine after contact with a lumberjack. He tried to get his own back by giving his captain out lbw to a ball so unexciting that the bowler didn't even appeal, but this proved to be only a temporary victory. When two months later he was fit to play again, he was chosen as twelfth man for no fewer than five consecutive matches before being allowed back into the team, and he never gave his captain out lbw again. Come to that, he never went skiing again either.

The moral is simple. Stay away from your team unless you are fit and chosen to play.

The End of the Season causes Temporary Retirement that is unavoidable unless you happen to be good enough to play in sunnier parts during the English winter. I am not that good, and from my experience of a game of cricket in Surrey on 29 February 1976, I can also advise against coming out of retirement to play in England during the winter. However, being in mothballs for six months of the year creates its own opportunities, and it gives you plenty of time to become even more indispensable to the side than you were after that unlucky duck in the final game of the season. Use the time, seize the opportunities, make your place in next year's side completely safe.

What do Compleat Cricketers do in winter? This question, perhaps as hotly debated over the years as what happened to the *Marie Celeste* and who killed Cock Robin, can now be answered. They do three things. They organise next season's fixture list, they repair, paint and rebuild almost everything to do with their club, and they raise funds to pay for the repairs, the paint and the printing of the fixture cards. It is all such fun.

The organisation of next season's fixture list is the easiest of the chores in question. All you need is this year's fixture list, details of which division of your local league you have been relegated to, the names and addresses of all the Fixtures Secretaries of all your potential opponents, and a 512K megabyte mainframe computer to sort it all out. The fixture lists are not usually finalised until well into the New Year, by which time the wives and children of all the Fixtures Secretaries of all your potential opponents have decided the where and the when of the summer holdiays, enabling these Hon Secs (Fixt) to make sure that they are available for all their favourite games, but long gone for the difficult ones, the matches that will administer the *coup de grâce* to the averages of all those participating. The printing of the fixture list is quite another matter. This job is generally taken on by the member of the club who has access to duplicating machinery at his office, and it is a rare bonus for any team who has somebody in the printing or artists' materials trades amongst their number. Such a man can earn himself lifetime selection just by doing the Fixture List each season. One team we used to play against included a wicket-keeper who was also a sub-editor on the local paper. He used to include his team's fixture list in the paper on the third Thursday in April each year. Production costs were thereby eliminated and each member of the club had to spend 18p to get a Fixture List. The local paper's circulation figures were always good for the third Thursday in April. At the other end of the spectrum, one club had its fixture list printed by their purveyor of leg-breaks and googlies, who also produced the parish magazine. It was the only fixture list I ever saw with the name of the preacher listed against every Sunday game.

The hard physical labour of the winter is the repainting of the pavilion, the replumbing of the loos thereof, and the overhaul and repair of the mower, heavy roller and scoreboard. These jobs make the summer tasks of marking out the pitch and putting up the sightscreen seem trivial in comparison, so in the same way that the Compleat Cricketer has found ways of eliminating those warm-weather tasks from his repertoire, he should also cut the winter heavy labour out of his act. There will always be somebody who enjoys repairing, painting and building, so leave him to it.

What you need to do is to Raise Funds to pay for all the work that somebody else will volunteer to carry out.

The standard format for Fund-Raising is to run a marathon or hang-glide from here to Aberdeen and back, and be sponsored in this activity to the extent of 5p a mile or some such. This serves the purpose not only of raising a certain amount of cash, perhaps enough to go halves on a paintbrush, but also of increasing dramatically the physical fitness level of the fund raisers. As we have seen in Chapter 8, this is not the correct approach as it may merely serve to eliminate the Nagging Injury. Even worse, it may create a real injury, necessitating further Temporary Retirement, and all the evils that accompany that state. So cut out the marathons and the hang-gliding and switch to other methods of filling the club piggy bank.

A far more satisfactory way of raising money is to shake a cocoa-tin in every pub from here to Grimsby. If you already live in Grimsby, then shake your cocoa-tin in every pub from Grimsby to here, and you will find that life really does exist on both sides of the Humber. All you do is ask for donations from all the patrons of the pub, and move on to the next place when your cocoa-tin is full. Common courtesy involves the sampling of the wares of each inn you enter, which explains why the percentage of funds raised which are promptly reinvested in further fund-raising activities is perhaps higher than with more abstemious organisations like Oxfam and Save The Children Fund. The added bonus is that after a couple of months of dedicated fund-raising the fitness of the cocoa-tin shaker will be at the correct level for an enjoyable season ahead.

Another method of fund-raising was used with some success by a colleague who worked in the head office of a large multinational corporation. In January one year, he sent a large envelope round his office asking for contributions to a present for Tracey Wrigglesworth of Accounts (Gen & Admin), who was leaving to have a baby. Despite the fact that Ms Wrigglesworth existed only in the imagination of our no. 8 batsman (who also bowls deceptively slowly as eighth change and fields whenever possible at eighth slip), the collection raised £32.49, two buttons and a wad of second-hand chewing gum. Messages of congratulation were attached from the managing director (who was clearly worried that he might be the father), the personnel director and the chief accountant. I must confess that we found these messages inappropriate when applied to the overhaul of our lawn-mower, but we put the rest of the collection to good use. The money bought a round or two at the Ploughman's Arms to put the mower repair gang into the right mood for their task. The buttons were useful additions to my jumble sale cricket flannels, and the chewing gum replaced a stud that went missing in action during the second game of the season.

Mention of my jumble sale cricket flannels would normally lead to cross-reference in the Index under 'Derision, Hoots of', but in this particular instance they lead me smoothly on to the subject of jumble sales. Jumble sales are a central feature of the Compleat Cricketer's winter and I am forced to confess that I wish they were not. Are there no more satisfactory ways of raising the money required to buy a new club box and repaint the number 7 on the telegraph? (Why repaint it at all when it looks so like a 1 that we actually won a match last season with a total 5 less than our opponents?) Did the vicar not know what he was doing when he bought Mrs Harcourt-Fanshawe's fruit cake, or did he really need a doorstop for the vestry? Is the brightly-painted pavilion, four-speed gang mower and enough left over to pay the petrol bill for five cars to Cornwall and back honestly worth the purgatory of the fund-raising jumble sale? I think not.

Over the years I believe I have attended even more jumble sales than I have scored unbeaten fifties, and yet I can count on the fingers of one hand the number of useful items I have purchased. Two pairs white flannels, one cup of tea and a mint condition *Eagle Annual No. 7*, and then my list comes to an abrupt halt. That is not to say that I have purchased nothing else at these ghastly events, which resemble nothing so much as an attempt to break the world records for Most People Packed Into A Village Hall and for Biggest Outbreak Of Mass Hysteria simultaneously. At the average jumble sale, there is the chance to spend your money on a wide range of totally unsaleable articles. The fact that otherwise sensible citizens seize this chance and part with hard-earned coins of the realm for the privilege of shuffling off home laden with all sorts of dross makes me despair for the future of mankind, but I too am gripped by this lemming-like mentality as soon as I go through the doors (10p per adult, 5p per child) and into the sale. How otherwise can I explain my outlay of 5p for a signed photograph of local personality Gerry Gable? What sensible man would cough up 20p for a pot plant that was clearly dead on arrival? Where is the point in buying back a paperback (*The Daily Telegraph 10th Crossword Puzzle Book*) which I donated to the sale in the first place? Why did I buy a broken radio for £2 when I have no interest in radio repairs and have six working sets at home already? Why did I spend 10p at the Kisses For Sale stall, when the lady selling the kisses was my own wife, who usually charges me less than 10p per kiss at home? I suppose that particular outlay was because I felt sorry for her (the stall finally raised 46p, thanks to the postman being given discount rates for quantity purchases), but the other items all sat in a pile at home until it was time for the next jumble sale, when they went off for somebody else to snap them up while the balance of the mind is disturbed.

I will admit that this is the only virtue of jumble sales — the opportunity it presents to get rid of the unwanted items that clutter every cupboard, every bottom drawer and every bookshelf in my household. I have successfully off-loaded a scratched copy of *The Black And White Minstrels No. 2* EP, a yellow waistcoat given to me by my grandmother one Christmas almost twenty years ago, a large number of almost new toys and a Monopoly set with the title deeds to Mayfair and Fenchurch St Station missing. My main failure (apart from *The Daily Telegraph 10th Crossword Puzzle Book*) was in giving away a vase my great-aunt had left me in her will, only to win it back as second prize in the raffle. I suspect supernatural intervention by my late great-aunt in this particular case, as she was never one to let her relatives get away with doing things of which she disapproved. The only consolation was that first prize was even less desirable — dinner for two at The Ploughman's Arms. Dinner for one is bad enough, but unless you wish to destroy a long-lasting relationship, deliberately inflicting that dinner on somebody else as well is not a good idea.

Let us move on from jumble sales, sadder but wiser. A far more enjoyable form of fund-raising is the cricket dinner. Steak and kidney pie for forty at any local hostelry (apart from the Ploughman's Arms), a guest speaker and plenty of beer to drink and bread rolls to throw — what more can a man ask for on a dark winter's night? If the truth be told, not a lot of money is raised, but plenty of glasses are, and that is half the battle. Speaking at the cricket dinner requires no little skill and concentration, and for the inexperienced the anticipation can destroy the appetite for what is usually a very acceptable blow-out. However, after considerable experience of both the giving and receiving of speeches at these functions, I have come to the conclusion that listening is harder than talking. The waiting is a harrowing experience. Will the speaker be:

a) witty;
b) dull;
c) loud;
d) inaudible;
e) long;
f) short;
g) drunk;
h) sober?

The combination of b), c), e) and g) is unfortunately the most regularly encountered, and frankly I'd rather be on the receiving end of a Dennis Lillee yorker than a speech like that. The most obvious reason for the Compleat Cricketer to make a speech is one of acceptance when the major awards for the season gone by are handed out. At the very least, after ten chapters of reading, marking, learning and inwardly digesting, you should stand a good chance of winning the Best Dressed Cricketer award. A couple of drinks for the captain at the bar before the meal should tie up the Most Valuable Player nomination as well, so have your acceptance speech ready. Make it brief. Anything longer than forty-five minutes tends to make people a little restive. My

'... anything longer than forty-five minutes...'

normal policy is to talk through my longest innings of the year, giving a ball-by-ball commentary to my listening public. This often takes as long as one minute forty-eight seconds, and then I can get back to throwing rolls at the other speakers. Luckily for them, I never win the award for Strongest Throwing Arm. But then there's always next season....

Let us turn away now from those for whom there is a next season, and study the particular problems of the Permanently Retired. The man who has handed in his box, sold his bat and wears his cricket flannels to do the gardening — what does the future hold for him? Well, very little actually, but I'd like to break it gently as this can come as a bit of a shock to those who thought that retirement from cricket was but another small step in the journey of life.

The only reason that anybody ever voluntarily gives up playing cricket is Old Age, and with the many standards of cricket available up and down the country, crumbling senility usually gets to a man at least two seasons before he needs to think about giving up cricket. But when that day finally comes, what is left in life?

There are two big joys still available to the man who, to paraphrase T.S. Eliot's immortal lines, has done with birth and copulation but is still studiously avoiding death. The first of the two is Umpiring, and the other is Committee Work.

Chapter 6 (VI) has already dealt at nauseating length with the intricacies of umpiring, and I am certainly not going to give an encore here. It will be noticed, however, by those of you who wish to flip back a page or two, that that particular section began with the qualifying clauses 'Whenever two impartial umpires are not available at the start of a match'. Sometimes two impartial umpires are available, and these fine fellows often come from the ranks of the Permanently Retired. There is a vast difference between an umpire who is a player waiting to bat and an umpire who is there to umpire. As we have seen, the player waiting to bat wants to carry on playing for his team for a few more years yet, which limits the range of decisions available to him when standing in judgement over his team-mates. The umpire who is there to umpire is as a rule greeted with such eagerness by the players who see one less chore ahead of them, that he can be confident of umpiring again next week and forever if he wants to. This is power. The gloves are off and the umpire can be bloody, bold and resolute with impunity. Despite the fact that umpires of this ilk have often been forced to give up playing because of failing eyesight, delirium tremens and terminal incontinence, players will be happy to abide by their decisions just to avoid having to stand there all afternoon themselves.

Permanent Retirement also gives a man the opportunity to spend his declining years in service to his club as a Good Committee Man. In the late 1960s and early 1970s Radio Hanoi (everybody's favourite Easy Listening Station) used to describe the US forces in Vietnam as 'The U.S. Aggressor Troops'. They were never merely 'The US Army' or 'The Enemy' or even 'The US Troops'. They were always 'The US Aggressor Troops'. The words were indivisible from each other. The same is true of the Good Committee Man. Nobody is ever a Bad Committee Man or even just a Committee Man. Cricket clubs only have Good Committee Men, and many of them come from the ranks of the Permanently Retired.

There is actually nothing difficult about becoming a Good Committee Man. The news editors at Radio Hanoi will, as I have implied, vouch for the fact that just being elected to a committee gives a man an absolute right to the title of Good Committee Man and being elected to the committee of your local cricket club could hardly be easier. All you do is turn up at the Annual General Meeting and unless you kick, scream and fight against it, hey presto! you are elected to the committee. Good Committee Men have lots of things to do, like Organising, Selecting and Blackballing, and, if there is no other way a man can get out of the house during his final slide into senile dementia and ultimate organic decay, he can do worse than sit on his Cricket Club Committee.

There are inevitably disadvantages to life as a GCM. For a start, among your peers you will find people still active in the game (e.g. the Club Captain) who for no sound reason believe that their views should carry more weight than those of an elderly buffoon who couldn't tell a cricket bat from a vampire bat unless it got up and bit him. Secondly, your wife will occasionally express reluctance at being asked for the third time in four Sundays to Do The Teas. There will be days when the lot of a GCM is far from G. But do not despair! Remember you have time on your side. While all the young, agile members of your committee are out earning a living from 9 to 5 each weekday, you will be giving your individual attention to the main problems at hand, viz. how to build your power base and make sure that your views carry the day.

The GCM who is Permanently Retired has by his own hand eliminated himself from the struggles of the game itself. For him the days of jockeying for the no. 7 position in the batting order are ancient history. No more for him the petty successes of being asked to field under the lime trees on the hottest afternoon of the summer, nor of avoiding paying for the tea for a third consecutive weekend. Now it is the real thing, the Main Board of the Business of Cricket.

The two greatest positions of power on the cricket club committee are unquestionably those of Secretary and of Keeper of the Club Records. As a general rule, Secretary is the least sought-after job on the Committee as it actually involves a considerable amount of work. But then a faint heart never won a fair maid. The Secretary may have to spend an excessive proportion of his waking hours writing letters, minutes and agendas but how else is an ex-cricketer going to fill in the time between breakfast and bedtime? The advantages of being Secretary are too many to list in their entirety, but the most obvious plus point is the absolute control that he has over the running of the club. He writes the minutes of each meeting, his version of what happened and what is to happen is the authorised version, and he co-ordinates the activities of all parts of the club in the manner that best suits him. Compared to the Secretary, the President and the Captain are but minor nobility at the court of Ivan the Terrible.

The Keeper of the Club Records has opportunities as well, but his power is based on days gone by. The first thing any GCM entrusted with the Club Records should do is to volunteer to write a History of the Club. This will be greeted with enthusiasm by all fellow committee members, and indeed all those associated with the Club, for after all, any hint of possible public acclaim is enough to turn the heads of even the most dour and defensive of cricketers. No deadline must be put on the completion of this History, as this involves a bluff being called. It is always possible to delay things by saying that it is proving more complicated than originally expected, or that a crucial volume of the scorebooks for 1937 are missing. In the meantime power is built up by dropping little historical facts into the conversation at the right moments.

'That match against Lower Scoring in 1964 was an interesting one,' says the putative historical author to his captain. 'I'll be dealing with it in detail in the History. Pity you were out first ball that day.'

Or 'Amazing that my little partnership with Jim for the ninth wicket, against St Dunstan's Old Boys in June 71, is still the club record.' These things can disconcert, and while you keep the Club Records there is nobody to gainsay you. The Keeper of the Club Records also has the opportunity to restructure the Club Records, if he failed to do so during his playing days when co-opted as Scorer (see Chapter 6). A playing career that at the time seemed notable only for the consistent brevity of its constituent parts can be turned into a yardstick for all current and future players, by the simple expedient of constructive reinterpretation of the historical facts, i.e. generous wielding of the rubber. By the time the Club History is ready for the presses, it will contain details of a playing career second only to W.G.Grace in all-round brilliance.

It might be thought that being Treasurer is the real seat of Club power, but this is not so. The Treasurer handles the cash, and since honesty is the standard characteristic of the Compleat Cricketer, he can do nothing but collect it and spend it in the way his fellow committee men direct. Accounts can of course be massaged, manipulated and manoeuvred in a way that any chartered accountant will unhesitatingly assert is a million miles away from fiddling, but the average cricket club with an annual turnover of say £1500 does not afford the opportunity for embezzlement on the grand scale, so, unless you can make enough money to make a clean escape and a new life in a country with which Britain has no extradition treaty, why bother? Even then, be warned. Her Majesty's Government have, at the latest count, extradition agreements with all nations in which cricket is played, so it has to be a straight choice between massive ill-gotten gains or a life revolving around cricket. The decision is simple, which is why Cricket Club Treasurers are always entirely trustworthy, and entirely powerless.

A final joy for the Permanently Retired, whether GCM or not, is in the giving of advice. Nothing makes an elderly heart leap with innocent pleasure as much as the expression on the face of a cricketer given out lbw for 2 to whom the advice, 'I'd have played forward to that one,' has been given. This passing-on of the experience of a lifetime to a future generation of cricketers is what it's all about.

'Was the sun in your eyes then?' is the sort of remark that can be made on an overcast day to a fielder who has missed a sitter at square leg. Watch then how the fielder's eyes will light up, and he will begin to mutter something under his breath, probably some indistinct speech of thanks for the advice rendered. Those few kindly words have not been in vain.

All the same, retirement is not easy. Some men forsake cricket altogether and take up bowls or bridge. Some men put a regular pattern on their boredom by swimming 30 lengths of the pool each morning. Some men take the easy way out and drop dead before their retirement has really got started. But if you really can't face it, there is one further option. You could always make a comeback. All that involves is turning back to Chapter 1 and living happily ever after.

'... retirement is not easy...'